THE BRAINDEAD MEGAPHONE

ESSAYS

GEORGE SAUNDERS

RIVERHEAD BOOKS

New York

RIVERHEAD BOOKS
Published by the Penguin Group
Penguin Group (USA) Inc.
375 Hudson Street, New York, New York 10014, USA
Penguin Group (Canada), 90 Eglinton Avenue East, Suite 700, Toronto,
Ontario M4P 2Y3, Canada (a division of Pearson Penguin Canada Inc.)
Penguin Books Ltd., 80 Strand, London WC2R 0RL, England
Penguin Group Ireland, 25 St. Stephen's Green, Dublin 2, Ireland
(a division of Penguin Books Ltd.)
Penguin Group (Australia), 250 Camberwell Road, Camberwell,
Victoria 3124, Australia (a division of Pearson Australia Group Pty. Ltd.)
Penguin Books India Pvt. Ltd., 11 Community Centre, Panchsheel Park,
New Delhi—110 017, India
Penguin Group (NZ), 67 Apollo Drive, Rosedale, North Shore 0745,
Auckland, New Zealand (a division of Pearson New Zealand Ltd.)
Penguin Books (South Africa) (Pty.) Ltd., 24 Sturdee Avenue, Rosebank,
Johannesburg 2196, South Africa

Penguin Books Ltd., Registered Offices: 80 Strand,
London WC2R 0RL, England

Some of these pieces have appeared, often in substantially different form,
in GQ, the Guardian, McSweeney's, the New Yorker, Slate, on Amazon.com,
in the anthologies Take My Advice, Best American Travel Writing, and Best
American Non-Required Reading, and as the introduction for the Modern
Library paperback edition of Adventures of Huckleberry Finn.

Cover design by Rodrigo Corral; Cover art by Getty Images
Book design by Judith Stagnitto Abbate/Abbate Design

First Riverhead trade paperback edition: September 2007

Library of Congress Cataloging-in-Publication Data

Saunders, George, 1958—
The braindead megaphone / George Saunders.—1st Riverhead
trade pbk. ed.
p. cm.
ISBN 978-1-59448-256-4
I. Title.
PS3569.A7897B73 2007
813'.54—dc22
2007006410

PRINTED IN THE UNITED STATES OF AMERICA

10   9   8   7   6   5   4   3   2

*To my parents, on the occasion of their
fiftieth wedding anniversary, with gratitude
for their beautiful example.*

CONTENTS

THE BRAINDEAD MEGAPHONE

1.

I find myself thinking of a guy standing in a field in the year 1200 doing whatever it is people in 1200 did while standing in fields. I'm thinking about his mind, wondering what's in it. What's he talking about in that tape-loop in his head? Who's he arguing with? From whom is he defending himself, to whom is he rationalizing his actions?

I'm wondering, in other words, if his mental experience of life is different in any essential way from mine.

What I have in common with this guy, I suspect, is that a lot of our mental dialogue is with people we know: our parents, wives, kids, neighbors.

Where I suspect we part ways is in the number and nature of the conversations we have with people we've never met.

He probably does some talking to his gods, his ancestors, mythological beings, historical figures. So do I. But there is a category of people I mentally converse with that he does not: people from far away, who've arrived in the mind, with various agendas, via high-tech sources.

I suspect that you also have these people in your mind; in fact, as you read this (sorry, sorry) I am become one of them.

Is this difference between us and Mr. or Ms. 1200 a good thing or a bad thing? I'm not sure. For now, let's just acknowledge it as a *difference*; a change in what human beings are asking their minds to do on a daily basis.

2.

Imagine a party. The guests, from all walks of life, are not negligible. They've been around: they've lived, suffered, own businesses, have real areas of expertise. They're talking about things that interest them, giving and taking subtle correction. Certain submerged concerns are coming to the surface and—surprise, pleasant surprise—being confirmed and seconded and assuaged by other people who've been feeling the same way.

Then a guy walks in with a megaphone. He's not the smartest person at the party, or the most experienced, or the most articulate.

But he's got that megaphone.

Say he starts talking about how much he loves early mornings in spring. What happens? Well, people turn to listen. It would be hard not to. It's only polite. And soon, in their small groups, the guests may find themselves talking about early spring mornings. Or, more correctly, about the validity of Megaphone Guy's ideas about early spring mornings. Some are agreeing with him, some disagreeing—but because he's so loud, their conversations will begin to react to what he's saying. As he changes topics, so do they. If he continually uses the phrase "at the end of the day," they start using it too. If he weaves into his arguments the assumption that the west side of the room is preferable to the east, a slow westward drift will begin.

These responses are predicated not on his intelligence, his unique experience of the world, his powers of contemplation, or his ability with language, but on the volume and omnipresence of his narrating voice.

His main characteristic is his *dominance*. He crowds the other voices out. His rhetoric becomes the central rhetoric because of its unavoidability.

In time, Megaphone Guy will ruin the party. The guests will stop believing in their value as guests, and come to see their main role as reactors-to-the-Guy. They'll stop doing what guests are supposed to do: keep the conversation going per their own interests and concerns. They'll become passive, stop believing in the validity of their own impressions. They may not even notice they've started speaking in his diction, that their thoughts are being limned by his. What's important to him will come to seem important to them.

We've said Megaphone Guy isn't the smartest, or most articulate, or most experienced person at the party—but what if the situation is even worse than this?

Let's say he hasn't carefully considered the things he's saying. He's basically just blurting things out. And even with the megaphone, he has to shout a little to be heard, which limits the complexity of what he can say. Because he feels he has to be entertaining, he jumps from topic to topic, favoring the conceptual-general ("We're eating more cheese cubes—and loving it!"), the anxiety- or controversy-provoking ("Wine running out due to shadowy conspiracy?"), the gossipy ("Quickie rumored in south bathroom!"), and the trivial ("Which quadrant of the party room do YOU prefer?").

We consider speech to be the result of thought (we have a thought, then select a sentence with which to express it), but thought also results from speech (as we grope, in words, toward meaning, we discover what we think). This yammering guy has, by forcibly putting his restricted language into the heads of the guests, affected the quality and coloration of the thoughts going on in there.

He has, in effect, put an intelligence-ceiling on the party.

3.

A man sits in a room. Someone begins shouting through his window, informing him of conditions in the house next door. Our man's mind inflects: that is, he begins imagining that house. What are the factors that might affect the quality of his imagining? That is, what factors affect his ability to imagine the next-door house as it actually *is*?

(1) The clarity of the language being used by the Informant (the less muddled, inarticulate, or jargon-filled, the better);

(2) The agenda of the Informant (*no agenda* preferable to *agenda-rich*);

(3) The time and care the Informant has spent constructing his narrative (i.e., the extent to which his account was revised and improved before being transmitted, with *more* time and care preferable to *less*);

(4) The time allowed for the communication (with *more* time preferable to *less*, on the assumption that more time grants the Informant a better opportunity to explain, explore, clarify, etc.).

So the best-case scenario for acquiring a truthful picture of that house next door might go something like this: Information arrives in the form of prose written and revised over a long period of time, in the interest of finding the truth, by a disinterested person with real-world experience in the subject area. The report can be as long, dense, nuanced, and complex as is necessary to portray the complexity of the situation.

The worst-case scenario might be: Information arrives in the form of prose written by a person with little or no firsthand experience in the subject area, who hasn't had much time to revise what he's written, working within narrow time constraints, in the service of an agenda that may be subtly or overtly distorting his ability to tell the truth.

Could we make this worst-case scenario even worse? Sure. Let it be understood that the Informant's main job is to entertain and that, if he fails in this, he's gone. Also, the man being informed? Make him too busy, ill-prepared, and distracted to properly assess what the Informant's shouting at him.

Then propose invading the house next door.

Welcome to America, circa 2003.

4.

To my way of thinking, something latent in our news media became overt and catastrophic around the time of the O. J. Simpson trial. Because the premise of the crime's national importance was obviously false, it had to be bolstered. A new style of presentation had to be invented. To wring thousands of hours of coverage from what could have been summarized in a couple of minutes every few weeks, a new rhetorical strategy was developed, or—let's be generous—evolved.

If someone has to lecture ten hours a day on a piece of dog crap in a bowl, adjustments will need to be made. To say the ridiculous things that will need to be said to sustain the illusion that the dog-crap story is serious news ("Dog-crap expert Jesse Toville provides his assessment of the probable size of the dog and its psychological state at time-of-crappage!"), distortions of voice, face, and format will be required.

This erosion continued through the Monica Lewinsky scandal ("More at five about The Stain! Have you ever caused a Stain? Which color do you think would most effectively hide a Stain? See what our experts predicted you would say!"), and dozens of lesser (?) cases and scandals, all morbid, sensational, and blown out of proportion, often involving minor celebrities—and then came 9/11.

By this time our national discourse had been so degraded—our national language so dumbed-down— that we were sitting ducks. In that hour of fear and need, finding in our hands the set of crude, hyperbolic tools we'd been using to discuss O.J., et al., we began using them to decide whether to invade another country, and soon were in Bagdhad, led by Megaphone Guy, via "Countdown to Slapdown in the Desert!" and "Twilight for the Evil One: America Comes Calling!" Megaphone Guy, it seemed, had gone a little braindead. Or part of him had. What had gone dead was the curious part that should have been helping us *decide* about the morality and intelligence of invasion, that should have known that the war being discussed was a real war, that might actually happen, to real, currently living people. Where was our sense of agonized wondering, of real doubt? We got (to my memory) a lot of discussion of tactics (which route, which vehicles) and strategy (how would it "play on the Arab street") but not much about the essential morality of invasion. (We did not hear, for example, "Well, Ted, as Gandhi once said, 'What difference does it make to the dead, the orphans, and the homeless, whether the mad destruction is wrought under the name of totalitarianism or the holy name of liberty or democracy?'")

Am I oversimplifying here? Yes. Is all our media stupid? Far from it. Were intelligent, valuable things written about the rush to war (and about O.J. and Monica, and then Laci Peterson and Michael Jackson, et al.)? Of course.

But: Is some of our media very stupid? Hoo boy. Does stupid, near-omnipresent media make us more tolerant toward stupidity in general? It would be surprising if it didn't.

Is human nature such that, under certain conditions, stupidity can come to dominate, infecting the brighter quadrants, dragging everybody down with it?

5.

Last night on the local news I watched a young reporter standing in front of our mall, obviously freezing his ass off. The essence of his report was, Malls Tend to Get Busier at Christmas! Then he reported the local implications of his investigation: (1) This Also True at Our Mall! (2) When Our Mall More Busy, More Cars Present in Parking Lot! (3) The More Cars, the Longer It Takes Shoppers to Park! and (shockingly): (4) Yet People Still Are Shopping, Due to, It Is Christmas!

It sounded like information, basically. He signed off crisply, nobody back at NewsCenter8 or wherever laughed at him. And across our fair city, people sat there and took it, and I believe that, generally, they weren't laughing at him either. They, like us in our house, were used to it, and consented to the idea that some Informing had just occurred. Although what we had been told, we already knew, although it had been told in banal language, revved up with that strange TV-news emphasis ("cold WEATHer leads SOME motorISTS to drive less, CARrie!"), we took it, and, I would say, it did something to us: made us dumber and more accepting of slop.

Furthermore, I suspect, it subtly degraded our ability to make bold, meaningful sentences, or laugh at stupid, ill-considered ones. The next time we felt tempted to say something like, "Wow, at Christmas the malls sure do get busier due to more people shop at Christmas because at Christmas so many people go out to buy things at malls due to Christmas being a holiday on which gifts are given by some to others"—we might actually say it, this sentiment having been elevated by our having seen it all dressed-up on television, in its fancy faux-Informational clothing.

And next time we hear someone saying something like, "We are pursuing this strategy because other strategies, when we had considered them, we concluded that, in terms of overall effectiveness, they were not sound strategies, which is why we enacted the one we are now embarked upon, which our enemies would like to see us fail, due to they hate freedom," we will wait to see if the anchorperson cracks up, or chokes back a sob of disgust, and if he or she does not, we'll feel a bit insane, and therefore less confident, and therefore more passive.

There is, in other words, a cost to dopey communication, even if that dopey communication is innocently intended.

And the cost of dopey communication is directly proportional to the omnipresence of the message.

6.

In the beginning, there's a blank mind. Then that mind gets an idea in it, and the trouble begins, because the mind mistakes the idea for the world. Mistaking the idea for the world, the mind formulates a theory and, having formulated a theory, feels inclined to act.

Because the idea is always only an approximation of the world, whether that action will be catastrophic or beneficial depends on the distance between the idea and the world.

Mass media's job is to provide this simulacra of the world, upon which we build our ideas. There's another name for this simulacra-building: storytelling.

Megaphone Guy is a storyteller, but his stories are not so good. Or rather, his stories are limited. His stories have not had time to gestate—they go out too fast and to too broad an audience. Storytelling is a language-rich enterprise, but Megaphone Guy does not have time to generate powerful language. The best stories proceed from a mysterious truth-seeking impulse that narrative has when revised extensively; they are complex and baffling and ambiguous; they tend to make us slower to act, rather than quicker. They make us more humble, cause us to empathize with people we don't know, because they help us imagine these people, and when we imagine them—if the storytelling is good enough—we imagine them as being, essentially, like us. If the story is poor, or has an agenda, if it comes out of a paucity of imagination or is rushed, we imagine those other people as essentially unlike us: unknowable, inscrutable, inconvertible.

Our venture in Iraq was a literary failure, by which I mean a failure of imagination. A culture better at imagining richly, three-dimensionally, would have had a greater respect for war than we did, more awareness of the law of unintended consequences, more familiarity with the world's tendency to throw aggressive energy back at the aggressor in ways he did not expect. A culture capable of imagining complexly is a humble culture. It acts, when it has to act, as late in the game as possible, and as cautiously, because it knows its own girth and the tight confines of the china shop it's blundering into. And it knows that no matter how well-prepared it is—no matter how ruthlessly it has held its projections up to intelligent scrutiny—the place it is headed for is going to be very different from the place it imagined. The shortfall between the imagined and the real, multiplied by the violence of one's intent, equals the evil one will do.

7.

So how did we get here? I think it went something like this: Elements on the right (Fox News, Rush Limbaugh, etc.) resuscitated an old American streak of simplistic, jingoistic, fear-based rhetoric that, in that post-9/11 climate of fear, infected, to a greater or lesser extent, the rest of the media. Remember Bill O'Reilly interrupting/chastising/misrepresenting Jeremy Glick, whose father died on 9/11, finally telling Glick to shut up, cutting off his microphone? And a few months later, Diane Sawyer's strange Mother Confessor interview/interrogation of the Dixie Chicks?

Ah, those were the days.

But also, those *are* the days, and the days yet to come. The basic illness in our media is not cured; it's only that our fear has subsided somewhat. When the next attack comes, the subsequent swing to the Stalinesque will be even more extreme, having, as it will, the additional oomph of retrospective repentance of what will then be perceived as a period (i.e., *now*) of relapse to softness and terror-encouraging open discourse.

Have we gone entirely to hell? No: the media, like life, is complex and stratified, filled with heroes holding the line. (All hail Bill Moyers; all hail Soledad O'Brien, post-Katrina, losing her temper with FEMA Director Michael Brown.) But if we define the Megaphone as *the composite of the hundreds of voices we hear each day that come to us from people we don't know, via high-tech sources*, it's clear that a significant and ascendant component of that voice has become bottom-dwelling, shrill, incurious, ranting, and agenda-driven. It strives to antagonize us, make us feel anxious, ineffective, and alone; convince us that the world is full of enemies and of people stupider and less agreeable than ourselves; is dedicated to the idea that, outside the sphere of our immediate experience, the world works in a different, more hostile, less knowable manner. This braindead tendency is viral and manifests intermittently; while it is the blood in the veins of some of our media figures, it flickers on and off in others. It frequently sheds its political skin for a stroll through Entertainment Park, where it leers and smirks and celebrates when someone is brought low by, say, an absence of underwear or a drunken evening.

But why should this tendency be ascendant? Fear, yes, fear is part of it. In a time of danger, the person sounding the paranoid continual alarm will eventually be right. A voice arguing for our complete rightness and the complete wrongness of our enemies, a voice constantly broadening the definition of "enemy," relieves us of the burden of living with ambiguity. The sensibility that generates a phrase like "unfortunate but necessary collateral damage" can, in the heat of the moment, feel like a kind of dark, necessary pragmatism.

But more than fear, our new braindeadedness has to do, I think, with commerce: the shift that has taken place within our major news organizations toward the corporate model, and away from the public-interest model. The necessity of profit is now assumed for our mass-media activities. This assumption has been shorn of all moral baggage: it is just something sophisticated people concede, so that other, more vital, discussions of "content" can begin.

Now, why aggressive, anxiety-provoking, maudlin, polarizing discourse should prove more profitable than its opposite is a mystery. Maybe it's a simple matter of drama: ranting, innuendo, wallowing in the squalid, the exasperation of the already-convinced, may, at some crude level, just be *more interesting* than some intelligent, skeptical human being trying to come to grips with complexity, especially given the way we use our media: as a time-killer in the airport, a sedative or stimulant at the end of a long day.

In any event, the people who used to ask, "Is it news?" now seem to be asking, "Will it stimulate?" And the change is felt, high and low, throughout the culture.

Imagine a village. A nearby village, having grown a surplus of a certain vegetable that, when eaten, turns the skin red, cuts our village a deal on this vegetable. Within a few months, the average color of the people in our village will have moved toward the Red end of the spectrum. Within that general trend will be all sorts of variations and exceptions: this guy eats as much as he likes of that vegetable but just goes a little Pink; this woman, who can't stand the taste of it, and never eats it, stays the same color as always. But in general, because of the omnipresence of that vegetable, the village is going to become Redder, and at the far end of the Gaussian curve folks will start looking downright demonic.

What, in this model, is the "vegetable"? What is "Red"?

The vegetable that has come to dominate our village is the profit motive.

"Red" is the resulting coarseness of our public rhetoric.

Now, profit is fine; economic viability is wonderful. But if these trump every other consideration, we will be rendered perma-children, having denied ourselves use of our higher faculties. With every grave-faced discussion of the disposition of the fetus within the body of its murdered mother, every interview with someone who knew the lawyer of an alleged close friend of some new Anna Nicole Smith, we become more clownish and bloated, and thereby more vulnerable.

In surrendering our mass storytelling function to entities whose first priority is profit, we make a dangerous concession: "Tell us," we say in effect, "as much truth as you can, *while still making money.*" This is not the same as asking: "Tell us the truth."

A culture's ability to understand the world and itself is critical to its survival. But today we are led into the arena of public debate by seers whose main gift is their ability to compel people to continue to watch them.

8.

The generalizing writer is like the passionate drunk, stumbling into your house mumbling: *I know I'm not being clear, exactly, but don't you kind of feel what I'm feeling?* If, generously overlooking my generalizations, your gut agrees with my gut in feeling that the nightly news may soon consist entirely of tirades by men so angry and inarticulate that all they do is sputter while punching themselves in the face, punctuated by videos of dogs blowing up after eating firecrackers, and dog-explosion experts rating the funniness of the videos—if you accept my basic premise that media is getting meaner and dumber—we might well ask, together: Who's running this mess? Who's making Sean Hannity's graphics? Who's booking the flights of that endless stream of reporters standing on the beach in the Bahamas, gravely speculating about the contents of a dead woman's stomach?

Well, that would be us. Who runs the media? Who *is* the media? The best and brightest among us—the most literate and ambitious and gifted, who go out from their homes and off to the best colleges, and from there to the best internships, and from there to offices throughout the nation, to inform us. They take the jobs they take, I suspect, without much consideration of the politics of their employer. What matters is the level of Heaven that employer occupies. The national is closer to God than the local; the large market looks down upon the small; the lately ratings-blessed floats slowly up, impressing the angels whose upward movement has fizzled out, because they work for losers.

There's no conspiracy at work, I don't think, no ill will, no leering Men Behind the Curtain: just a bunch of people from good universities, living out the dream, cringing a little at the dog-crap story even as they ensure that it goes out on time, with excellent production values.

How does such a harmful product emanate from such talented people? I'd imagine it has to do with the will to survive: each small piece of the machine doing what he or she must to avoid going home to Toledo, tail-between-legs, within the extant constraints of time and profitability, each deferring his or her "real" work until such time as he or she accumulates his or her nut and can head for the hills, or get a job that lets them honor their hearts. (A young friend who writes content for the news page of an online media giant, e-mails me: "I just wrote this news headline for my job: 'Anna Nicole's Lost Diary: "I Hate Sex."' If anyone wonders why Americans aren't informed with real news it's because of sell-out corporate goons like me who will do anything to never deliver a pizza again.")

An assistant to a famous conservative opinion-meister once described her boss to me, a little breathlessly and in the kind of value-neutral mode one hears in this milieu, as being one of the funniest, most intelligent, high-energy people she'd ever met. I believed her. To do what he does must take a special and terrifying skill set. Did she agree with his politics? She demurred—she did and she didn't. It was kind of beside the point. He was kicking much ass. I immediately felt a little gauche for asking about her politics, like a guy who, in the palace, asks how much the footman makes.

The first requirement of greatness is that one stay in the game. To stay in the game, one must prove viable; to prove viable, one has to be watched; to be watched, one has to be watchable, and, in the news business, a convention of Watchability has evolved—a tone, a pace, an unspoken set of acceptable topics and acceptable relations to these topics—that bears, at best, a peripheral relation to truth. What can be said on TV is circumscribed, subtly, by past performance, editing, and social cues, and, not so subtly, by whether one is invited back.

This entity I'm trying to unify under the rubric of The Megaphone is, of course, in reality, a community tens of thousands of people strong, and like all communities, it is diverse, and resistant to easy generality, and its ways are mysterious.

But this community constitutes a kind of *de facto* ruling class, because what it says we can't avoid hearing, and what we hear changes the way we think. It has become a kind of branch of our government: when government wants to mislead, it turns to the media; when media gets hot for a certain story (i.e., senses a ratings hot spot), it influences the government. This has always been true, but more and more this relationship is becoming a closed loop, which leaves the citizen extraneous. Like any ruling class, this one looks down on those it rules. The new twist is that this ruling class rules via our eyes and the ears. It fills the air, and thus our heads, with its priorities and thoughts, and its new stunted diction.

This is a ruling class made of strange bedfellows: the Conservative Opinion King has more in common with the Liberal Opinion King than either does with the liberal and conservative slaughterhouse workers toiling side by side in Wichita; the Opinion Kings have friends in common, similar ambitions, a common frame of reference (agents, expected perks, a knowledge of the hierarchy of success indicators, a mastery of insider jargon). What they share most is a desire not to be cast down, down from the realm of the rarefied air, back to where they came from.

There's a little slot on the side of the Megaphone, and as long as you're allowed to keep talking into it, money keeps dropping out.

Seasons pass. What once would have evoked an eyeroll evokes a dull blink. New truisms, new baselines, arise. A new foundation, labeled Our Basic Belief System, is laid, and on this foundation appear startling new structures: a sudden quasi acceptance of, say, the waterboarding of prisoners, or of the idea that a trial is a privilege we may choose to withhold if we deem the crime severe enough.

9.

At this point I hear a voice from the back of the room, and it is mine: "Come on, George, hasn't our mass media always been sensationalistic, dumb, and profit-seeking?"

Of course it has. If you want a tutorial on stupid tonality, watch an old newsreel ("These scrappy Southern Yanks are taking a brisk walk toward some Krauts who'll soon be whistling Dixie out of the other side of Das Traps!"). We were plenty able to whip ourselves into murderous frenzies even when the Megaphone was a baby, consisting of a handful of newspapers (Hi, Mr.

Hearst!), and I suppose if we went back far enough, we'd find six or seven troglodytes madly projecting about a village of opposing troglodytes, then jogging down there, hooting pithy slogans, to eliminate it on the fallacious power of their collective flame-fanning.

But I think we're in an hour of special danger, if only because our technology has become so loud, slick, and seductive, its powers of self-critique so insufficient and glacial. The era of the jackboot is over: the forces that come for our decency, humor, and freedom will be extolling, in beautiful smooth voices, the virtue of decency, humor, and freedom.

Imagine that the Megaphone has two dials: One controls the Intelligence of its rhetoric and the other its Volume. Ideally, the Intelligence would be set on High, and the Volume on Low—making it possible for multiple, contradictory voices to be broadcast and heard. But to the extent that the Intelligence is set on Stupid, and the Volume on Drown Out All Others, this is verging on propaganda, and we have a problem, one that works directly against the health of our democracy.

Is there an antidote?

Well, there is, but it's partial, and may not work, and isn't very exciting. Can we legislate against Stupidity? I don't think we'd want to. Freedom means we have to be free to be Stupid, and Banal, and Perverse, free to generate both *Absalom, Absalom!*, and *Swapping Pets: The Alligator Edition.* Freedom means that if some former radio DJ can wrestle his way to the top of the heap and provoke political upheavals by spouting his lame opinions and bullying his guests, he too has a right to have a breakfast cereal named after him. American creative energy has always teetered on the brink of insanity. "Rhapsody in Blue" and "The Night Chicago Died" have, alas, common

DNA, the DNA for "joyfully reckless confidence." What I propose as an antidote is simply: awareness of the Megaphonic tendency, and discussion of same. Every well-thought-out rebuttal to dogma, every scrap of intelligent logic, every absurdist reduction of some bullying stance is the antidote. Every request for the clarification of the vague, every poke at smug banality, every pen stroke in a document under revision is the antidote.

This battle, like any great moral battle, will be won, if won, not with some easy corrective tidal wave of Total Righteousness, but with small drops of specificity and aplomb and correct logic, delivered titrationally, by many of us all at once.

We have met the enemy and he is us, yes, yes, but the fact that we have recognized ourselves as the enemy indicates we still have the ability to rise up and whip our own ass, so to speak: keep reminding ourselves that representations of the world are never the world itself. Turn that Megaphone down, and insist that what's said through it be as precise, intelligent, and humanc as possible.

THE
NEW
MECCA

PUT THAT STATELY PLEASURE
PALACE THERE BETWEEN
THOSE OTHER TWO

If you are like I was before I went to Dubai, you may not know exactly where Dubai is. Near Venezuela? No, sorry, that is incorrect. Somewhere north of Pakistan, an idyllic mountain kingdom ruled by gentle goatherds? Well, no.

Dubai, actually, is in the United Arab Emirates, on the Arabian Peninsula, one hundred miles across the Gulf from Iran, about six hundred miles from Basra, eleven hundred from Kabul.

You might also not know, as I did not know, what Dubai is all about or why someone would want to send you there. You might wonder: Is it dangerous? Will I be beheaded? Will I need a translator? Will my translator be beheaded? Just before we're beheaded, will my translator try to get out of it by blaming everything on me?

No, no, not to worry. Dubai, turns out, is quite possibly the safest great city in the world. It is also the newest great city in the world. In the 1950s, before oil was discovered there, Dubai was just a cluster of mud huts and Bedouin tents along Dubai Creek: the entire city has basically been built in the last fifty years. And actually, the cool parts—the parts that have won Dubai its reputation as "the Vegas of the Middle East" or "the Venice of the Middle East" or "the Disney World of the Middle East, if Disney World were the size of San Francisco and out in a desert"—have been built in the last ten years. And the supercool parts—the parts that, when someone tells you about them, your attention drifts because these morons have to be lying (no one dreams this big or has that much available capital)—those parts are all going to be built in the next five years.

By 2010, if all goes according to plan, Dubai will have: the world's tallest skyscraper (2,300 feet), largest mall, biggest theme park, longest indoor ski run, most luxurious underwater hotel (accessible by submarine train); a huge (2,000-acre, 60,000-resident) development called International City, divided into nation-neighborhoods (England, China, France, Greece, etc.) within which all homes will be required to reflect the national architectural style; not to mention four artificially constructed island mega-archipelagoes (three shaped like giant palm trees, the fourth like a map of the world) built using a specially designed boat that dredges up tons of ocean-bottom sand each day and sprays it into place.

Before I saw Dubai for myself, I assumed this was bluster: brag about ten upcoming projects, finally build one—smaller than you'd bragged—hope everyone forgets about the other nine.

But no.

I've been to Dubai, and I believe.

If America was looking for a pluralistic, tax-free, laissez-faire, diverse, inclusive, tolerant, no-holds-barred, daringly capitalist country to serve as a shining City on the Hill for the entire Middle East, we should have left Iraq alone and sponsored a National Peaceful Tourist Excursion to Dubai and spent our ninety quadrillion Iraq War dollars there.

Maybe.

IN WHICH I FALL IN LOVE WITH
A FAKE TOWN

From the air, Dubai looked something like Dallas circa 1985: a vast expanse of one- or two-story white boxes, punctuated by clusters of freakish skyscrapers. (An Indian kid shouted, "Dad, looks like a microchip!") Driving in from the airport, you're struck by the usual first-night-in-new-country exotica ("There's a *Harley-Davidson* dealership—right in the *Middle East!*"), and the skyscraper clusters were, OK, odd-looking (like four or five architects had staged a weird-off, with unlimited funds)—but all in all, it was, you know, a city. And I wondered what all the fuss was about.

Then I got to my hotel.

The Madinat Jumeirah is, near as I can figure, a superresort consisting of three, or possibly six, luxury sub-hotels and two, or maybe three, clusters of luxury villas, spread out over about forty acres, or for all I know it was twelve sub-hotels and nine luxury-villa clusters—I really couldn't tell, so seamless and extravagant and confusing was all the luxury. The Madinat is themed to resemble an ancient Arabian village. But to say the

Madinat is themed doesn't begin to express the intensity and opulence and areal extent of the theming. The site is crisscrossed by 2.3 miles of fake creeks, trolled night and day by dozens of fake Arabian water taxis (*abras*) piloted by what I can only describe as fake Arabs because, though dressed like old-timey Arabs, they are actually young, smiling, sweet-hearted guys from Nepal or Kenya or the Philippines, who speak terrific English as they pilot the soundless electrical *abras* through this lush, created Arabia, looking for someone to take back to the lobby, or to the largest outdoor pool in the Middle East, or over to Trader Vic's, which is also themed and looks something like a mysterious ancient Casbah inexplicably filled with beautiful contemporary people.

And so, though my first response to elaborate Theming is often irony (Who *did* this? And *why*? Look at that *modern Exit sign* over that *eighteenth-century bedstead*. Haw!), what I found during my stay at the Madinat is that irony is actually my first response to tepid, lame Theming. In the belly of radical Theming, my first response was to want to stay forever, bring my family over, set up shop in my hut-evoking villa, and never go home again.

Because the truth is, it's beautiful. The air is perfumed, you hear fountains, the tinkling of bells, distant chanted prayers, and when the (real) Arabian moon comes up, yellow and attenuated, over a (fake) Arabian wind tower, you feel you are a resident of some ancient city—or rather, some ancient city if you had dreamed the ancient city, and the ancient city had been purged of all disease, death, and corruption, and you were a Founder/Elder of that city, much beloved by your Citizens, the Staff.

Wandering around one night, a little lost, I came to the realization that authenticity and pleasure are not causally related. How is this "fake"? This is real flow-

ing water, the date and palm trees are real, the smell of
incense and rose water is real. The staggering effect of
the immense scale of one particular crosswalk—which
joins two hotels together and is, if you can imagine this,
a four-story ornate crosswalk that looks like it should
have ten thousand cheering Imperial Troops clustered
under it and an enigmatic young Princess waving from
one of its arabesquey windows—that effect is *real*. You
feel it in your gut and your legs. It makes you feel happy
and heroic and a little breathless, in love anew with the
world and its possibilities. You have somehow entered
the landscape of a dream, the Platonic realization of the
idea of Ancient Village—but there are real smells here,
and when, a little dazzled, you mutter to yourself ("This
is like a freaking dream, I love it, I, wow . . ."), you don't
wake up, but instead a smiling Filipino kid comes up and
asks if you'd like a drink.

On the flight over, I watched an interview with an
employee of Jumeirah International, the company that
manages the Madinat. Even though he saw it going up
himself, he said, he feels it is an ancient place every time
he enters and finds it hard to believe that, three years
ago, it was all just sand.

A WORD ABOUT THE HELP

UAE nationals comprise about 20 percent of the city's
population. Until three years ago, only nationals were
allowed to own property in Dubai, and they still own
essentially all of it. Visually identifiable by their dress—
the men wear the traditional white dishdashas; the
women, long black gowns and abayas—these nationals
occupy the top rung of a rigid social hierarchy: imagine

Hollywood, if everyone who'd been wildly successful in the movie business had to wear a distinctive costume.

A rung down from the Emiratis are some two hundred thousand expats (mostly Brits but also other Europeans, Russians, Lebanese, Indians) who comprise a kind of managerial class: the marketing people, the hotel managers, the human-resource gurus, the accountants, the lawyers, etc. But the vast majority of Dubai's expat population—roughly two-thirds of it—comes from poorer countries all around the world, mainly South Asia or Africa. They built Dubai, they run it with their labor but can't afford to own homes or raise their families here. They take their dirhams home and cash them in for local currency, in this way increasing their wealth by as much as tenfold. They live here for two years, five years, fifteen years; take home-leaves as often as every three months or as infrequently as never.

And even within this class there are stratifications. The hotel workers I met at the Madinat, for example, having been handpicked by Jumeirah scouts from the finest hotels in their native countries, are a class, or two, or three, above the scores of South Asian laborers who do the heavy construction work, who live in labor camps on the outskirts of town where they sleep ten to a room, and whose social life, according to one British expat I met, consists of "a thrilling evening once a month of sitting in a circle popping their bulbs out so some bloody Russian chickie can race around hand-jobbing them all in a mob."

You see these construction guys all over town: somewhat darker-complexioned, wearing blue jumpsuits, averting their eyes when you try to say hello, squatting outside a work site at three in the morning because Dubai construction crews work twenty-four hours a day, seven days a week.

There is much to be done.

THE WILD WADI EPIPHANY

A short, complimentary golf-cart ride down the beach from the Madinat is Wild Wadi, a sprawling, themed water park whose theme is: a wadi is flooding! Once an hour, the sound of thunder/cracking trees/rushing waves blares through the facility-wide PA, and a waterfall begins dropping a thousand gallons of water a minute into an empty pond, which then violently overflows down the pedestrian walkways, past the gift shop.

Waiting in line, I'm part of a sort of United Nations of partial nudity: me, a couple of sunburned German women, three angry-looking Arab teens, kind of like the Marx Brothers if the Marx Brothers were Arabs in bathing suits with cigarettes behind their ears, who, I notice, are muttering to one another while glowering. Then I see what they're muttering/glowering about: several (like, fifteen) members of the United States Navy, on shore leave. You can tell they're Navy because they're huge and tattooed and innocently happy and keep bellowing things like, "Dude, fuck that, I am all *about* dancing!" while punching each other lovingly in the tattoos and shooting what I recognize as Rural Smiles of Shyness and Apprehension at all the people staring at them because they're so freaking loud.

Then the Navy Guys notice the Glowering Muttering Arabs, and it gets weirdly tense there in line. Luckily, it's my turn to awkwardly blop into a tube, and off I go.

This ride involves a series of tremendous water jets that blast you, on your tube, to the top of Wild Wadi, where, your recently purchased swim trunks having been driven up your rear by the jets, you pause, looking out over the entire city—the miles of stone-white villas, the Burj Al Arab (sail-shaped, iconic, the world's only seven-star hotel) out in the green-blue bay—just before you fly down so fast that you momentarily fear the next morning's headline will read "Middle-aged American Dies in Freak Waterslide Mishap; Bathing Suit Found Far Up Ass."

Afterward, I reconvene with my former line mates in a sort of faux river bend. Becalmed, traffic-jammed, we bob around in our tubes, trying to keep off one another via impotent little hand-flips, bare feet accidentally touching ("Ha, wope, sorry, heh . . ."), legs splayed, belly-up in the blinding 112-degree Arabian sun, self-conscious and expectant, as in: "Are we, like, stuck here? Will we go soon? I hope I'm not the one who drifts under that dang *waterfall* over there!"

No one is glowering or muttering now. We're sated, enjoying that little dopey buzz of quasi-accomplishment you feel after a surprisingly intense theme-park ride. One of the Arab kids, the one with the Chico hair, passes a drenched cigarette to me, to pass to his friend, and then a lighter, and suddenly everybody's smiling—me, the Arab Marxes, the sunburned German girls, the U.S. Navy.

A disclaimer: it may be that, when you're forty-six and pearl white and wearing a new bathing suit at a theme park on your first full day in Arabia, you're especially prone to Big Naive Philosophical Realizations.

Be that as it may, in my tube at Wild Wadi, I have a mini-epiphany: given enough time, I realize, statistically, despite what it may look like at any given moment, we *will* all be brothers. All differences will be bred out. There will be no pure Arab, no pure Jew, no pure American American. The old dividers—nation, race, religion—will be overpowered by crossbreeding and by our mass media, our world Culture o' Enjoyment.

Look what just happened here: hatred and tension were defused by Sudden Fun.

Still bobbing around (three days before the resort bombings in Cairo, two weeks after the London bombings), I think-mumble a little prayer for the great homogenizing effect of pop culture: same us out, Lord MTV! Even if, in the process, we are left a little dumber, please proceed. Let us, brothers and sisters, leave the intolerant, the ideologues, the religious Islamist Bolsheviks, our own solvers-of-problems-with-troops behind, fully clothed, on the banks of Wild Wadi. We, the New People, desire Fun and the Good Things of Life, and through Fun, we will be saved.

Then the logjam breaks, and we surge forward, down a mini-waterfall.

Without exception, regardless of nationality, each of us makes the same sound as we disappear: a thrilled little self-forgetting Whoop.

WE BUY, THEREFORE WE AM

After two full days of blissfully farting around inside the Madinat, I reluctantly venture forth out of the resort bubble, downtown, into the actual city, to the Deira souk. This is the real Middle East, the dark *Indiana Jones*–ish Middle East I'd preimagined: an exotic, cramped, hot, chaotic, labyrinthine, canopied street bazaar, crowded with room-size, even closet-size stalls, selling everything there is in the world to buy, and more than a few things you can't imagine anyone ever wanting to buy, or even accepting for free.

Here is the stall of Plastic Flowers That Light Up; the stall of Tall Thin Blond Dolls in Miniskirts with Improbably Huge Eyes; the stall of Toy Semiautomatic Weapons; the stall of Every Spice Known to Man (SARON BUKHOR, BAHRAT, MEDICAL HERBS, NATURAL VIAGRA); the stall of Coffee-Grinding Machines in Parts on the Floor; the stall of Hindi Prayer Cards; the stall of Spangled Kashmiri Slippers; of Air Rifles; Halloween Masks; Over-size Bright-Colored Toy Ships and Trucks; a stall whose walls and ceiling are completely covered with hundreds of cooking pots. There is a Pashtun-dominated section, a hidden Hindi temple, a section that suddenly goes Chinese, entire streets where nothing is sold but bolts of cloth. There's a mind-blowing gold section—two or three hundred gold shops on one street, with mysterious doors leading to four-story mini-malls holding still more gold shops, each overflowing with the yellow high-end gold that, in storybooks and Disney movies, comes pouring out of pirate chests.

As I walk through, a kind of amazed mantra starts running through my head: *There is no end to the making and selling of things there is no end to the making and selling of things there is no end . . .*

Man, it occurs to me, is a joyful, buying-and-selling piece of work. I have been wrong, dead wrong, when I've decried consumerism. Consumerism is what we are. It is, in a sense, a holy impulse. A human being is some-one who joyfully goes in pursuit of things, brings them home, then immediately starts planning how to get more.

A human being is someone who wishes to improve his lot.

SPEAKING OF IMPROVING ONE'S LOT: THE GREAT DUBAI QUANDARY

Dubai raises the questions raised by any apparent utopia: What's the downside? At whose expense has this nirvana been built? On whose backs are these pearly gates being raised?

Dubai is, in essence, capitalism on steroids: a small, insanely wealthy group of capital-controlling Haves supported by a huge group of overworked and underpaid Have-Nots, with, in Dubai's case, the gap between Haves and Have-Nots so wide as to indicate different species.

But any attempt to reduce this to some sort of sci-fi Masters and 'Droids scenario gets complicated. Relative to their brethren back home (working for next to nothing or not working at all), Dubai's South Asian workers have it great; likewise, relative to their brethren working in nearby Saudi Arabia. An American I met, who has spent the last fifteen years working in the Saudi oil industry, told me about seeing new South Indian workers getting off the plane in Riyadh, in their pathetic new clothes, clutching cardboard suitcases. On arrival, as in a scene out of *The Grapes of Wrath*, they are informed (for the first time) that they will have to pay for their flight over, their lodging, their food (which must be bought from the company), and, in advance, their flight home. In this way, they essentially work the first two years for free.

Dubai is not, in structure, much different: the workers surrender their passports to their employer;

there are no labor unions, no organizing, no protests. And yet in Dubai, the workers tell you again and again how happy they are to be here. Even the poorest, most overworked laborer considers himself lucky—he is making more, much more, than he would be back home. In Saudi, the windfall profits from skyrocketing oil prices have shot directly upstairs, to the five thousand or so members of the royal family, and from there to investments (new jets, real estate in London). In Dubai, the leaders have plowed the profits back into the national dream of the New Dubai—reliant not on oil revenue (the Dubai oil will be gone by 2010) but on global tourism. Whatever complaints you hear about the Emirati ruling class—they buy $250,000 falcons, squash all dissent, tolerate the financial presence of questionable organizations (Al Qaeda, various national Mafias)—they seem to be universally respected, even loved, because, unlike the Saudi rulers, they are perceived to put the interests of the people first.

On the other hand, relative to Western standards, Dubai is so antilabor as to seem medieval. In the local paper, I read about the following case: A group of foreign workers in Dubai quit their jobs in protest over millions of dirhams in unpaid wages. Since by law they weren't allowed to work for another company, these men couldn't afford plane tickets back home and were thus stuck in a kind of Kafka loop. After two years, the government finally stepped in and helped send the men home. This story indicates both the potential brutality of the system—so skewed toward the employer—and its flexibility relative to the Saudi system, its general right-heartedness, I think you could say, or at least its awareness of, and concern with, Western opinion: the situation was allowed to be reported and, once reported, was corrected.

Complicated.

Because you see these low-level foreign workers working two or three jobs, twelve, fourteen, sixteen hours a day, longing for home (a waiter shows me exactly how he likes to hold his two-year-old, or did like to hold her, last time he was home, eight months ago), and think: Couldn't you Haves cut loose with just a little more?

But ask the workers, in your intrusive Western way, about their Possible Feelings of Oppression, and they model a level of stoic noble determination that makes the Ayn Rand in you think, Good, good for you, sir, best of luck in your professional endeavors!

Only later, back in your room, having waded in through a lobby full of high rollers—beautifully dressed European/Lebanese/Russian expats, conferring Emiratis, all smoking, chatting, the expats occasionally making a scene, berating a waitress—thinking of some cabdriver in the thirteenth hour of his fourteen-hour shift, worrying about his distant grandchild; thinking of some lonely young Katmandu husband, sleeping fitfully in his sweltering rented room—do you get a sudden urge to move to Dubai and start a chapter of the Wobblies.

On the other hand:

A Kenyan security guard who works fourteen-hour days at Wild Wadi, euphoric about his new earning power, says to me: "I expect, in your writing, you will try to find the dark side of Dubai? Some positive, some negative? Isn't that the Western way? But I must say: I have found Dubai to be nearly perfect."

Complicated.

THE UNIVERSITY OF THE BACK
OF THE CAB

A partial list of wise things cabdrivers said to me in Dubai:

1) "If you good Muslim, you go straight, no talking talking, bomb blast! No. You go to mosque, to talk. You go straight!"
2) "This, all you see? So new! All new within! Within one year! Within within within! That building there? New within three year! All built within! Before, no! Only sand."
3) "You won't see any Dubai Arab man driving cab. Big boss only."
4) Re: the Taliban: "If you put a man into a room with no way out, he will fight his way out. But if you leave him one way out, he will take it."
5) "The Cyclone Club? Please to not go there. It is a disco known for too many fuck-girls."

One night my driver is an elderly Iranian, a fan of George W. Bush who hates the Iranian government. He tells me the story of his spiritual life. When young, he says, he was a donkey: a donkey of Islam. Then a professor said to him: You are so religious, so sure of yourself, and yet you know absolutely nothing. And this professor gave him books to read, from his personal library. "I read one, then more, more," he says, nearly moving himself to tears with the memory.

After two years, the driver had a revelation: All religious knowledge comes from the hand of man. God does not talk to us directly. One can trust only one's own mind, one's own intelligence. He has five kids, four grandkids, still works fourteen-hour days at sixty-five years old. But he stays in Dubai because in Iran, there are two classes: The Religious and The Not. And The Religious get all the privileges, all the money, all the best jobs. And if you, part of The Not Religious, say something against them, he says, they take you against a wall and . . .

He turns to me, shoots himself in the head with his finger.

As I get out, he says, "We are not different, all men are . . ." and struggles to remember the word.

"Brothers?" I say.

"No," he says.

"Unified?" I say.

"No," he says.

"Part of the same, uh . . . transcendent . . ."

"No," he says. He can't remember the word. He is old, very old, he says, sorry, sorry.

We say good-bye, promising to pray for our respective governments, and for each other.

CLEANING AMONG THE MAYHEM

Dubai is a city of people who come from elsewhere and are going back there soon. To start a good conversation—with a fellow tourist, with the help, with just about anybody—simply ask, "Where are you from?" Everyone wants to tell you. If white, they are usually from England, South Africa, or Ukraine. If not, they are from Sri Lanka, the Philippines, Kenya, Nepal, or India.

One hotel seems to hire only Nepalese. One bar has only Ukrainians. You discover a pocket of Sri Lankan golf-cart drivers, all anxious to talk about the tsunami.

One day, inexplicably, everyone you meet, wherever you go, is from the Philippines.

"Where are you from?" you say all day, and all day people brightly answer, "Philippines!"

That night, at a club called Boudoir, I meet L, an employee of Ford in Dubai, a manic, funny, Stanley Tucci–looking guy from Detroit, who welcomes me into his party, gets me free champagne, mourns the circa-1990 state of inner-city Detroit: feral dogs roaming the streets, trees growing out of the upper stories of skyscrapers where "you know, formerly, commerce was being done, the real 1960s automobile fucking world-class commerce, man!" The night kind of explodes. This, I think, this is the repressive Arabian Peninsula? Apparently, anything is permitted, as long as it stays within the space within which it is permitted. Here is a Palestinian who lives in L.A. and whose T-shirt says LAPD—WHERE EVERYBODY IS KING. A couple of blond Russian girls dance on a rail, among balloons. On the dance floor, two other blondes dance alone. A guy comes up behind one and starts passionately grinding her. This goes on awhile. Then he stops, introduces himself, she shakes his hand, he goes back to grinding her. His friend comes up, starts grinding her friend. I don't get it. Prostitutes? Some new youthful social code? I am possibly too old to be in here? The dance floor is packed, the whole place *becomes* the dance floor, the rails are now packed with dancers, a Lebanese kid petulantly shouts that if this was *fucking Beirut*, the girls would be *stripped off* by now, then gives me a snotty look and stomps away, as if it's my fault the girls are still dressed. I drop my wallet, look down, and see the tiniest little woman imaginable, with a whisk broom, struggling against the surge of the crowd like some kind of cursed Cleaning Fairy, trying to find a small swath of floor to sweep while being bashed by this teeming mass of gyrating International Hipsters. She's tiny—I mean *tiny*, like three feet tall, her head barely reaching all the gyrating waists—with thick glasses and bowl-cut hair.

Dear little person! It seems impossible she's trying to sweep the dance floor at a time like this; she seems uncommonly, heroically dedicated, like some kind of OCD janitor on the *Titanic*.

"Where are you from?" I shout.

"Philippines!" she shouts, and goes back to her sweeping.

MY ARRIVAL IN HEAVEN

The Burj Al Arab is the only seven-star hotel in the world, even though the ratings system only goes up to five. The most expensive Burj suite goes for twelve thousand dollars a night. The atrium is 590 feet from floor to ceiling, the largest in the world. As you enter, the staff rushes over with cold towels, rosewater for the hands, dates, incense. The smell, the scale, the level of loving, fascinated attention you are receiving, makes you realize you have never really been in the lap of true luxury before. All the luxury you have previously had—in New York, L.A.—was stale, Burj-imitative crap! Your entire concept of *being inside a building* is being altered in real time. The lobby of the Burj is neither inside nor out. The roof is so far away as to seem like sky. The underbellies of the floors above you grade through countless shades of color from deep blue to, finally, up so high you can barely see it: pale green. Your Guest Services liaison, a humble, pretty Ukrainian, tells you that every gold-colored surface you see during your stay is actual twenty-four-karat gold. Even those four-story columns? Even so, she says. Even the thick fourth-story arcs the size of buses that span the columns? All gold, sir, is correct.

I am so thrilled to be checking in! What a life! Where a kid from Chicago gets to fly halfway around the world and stay at the world's only seven-star hotel, and *GQ* pays for it!

But there was a difficulty.

HELP, HELP, HEAVEN IS MAKING ME NERVOUS

Because, for complicated reasons, *GQ* couldn't pay from afar, and because my wife and I share a common hobby of maxing out all credit cards in sight, I had rather naively embarked on a trip halfway around the world without an operative credit card: the contemporary version of setting sail with no water in the casks. So I found myself in the odd position of having to pay the off-season rate of fifteen hundred dollars a night, in cash. And because, turns out, to my chagrin, my ATM has a daily withdrawal limit (Surprise, dumb ass!), I found myself there in my two-floor suite (every Burj room is a two-story suite), wearing the new clothes I had bought back in Syracuse for the express purpose of "Arriving at the Burj," trying to explain, like some yokel hustler at a Motel 6 in Topeka, that I'd be happy to pay half in cash now, half on check-out, if that would be, ah, acceptable, would that be, you know, cool?

My God, if you could have bottled the tension there in my suite at the Burj! The absolute electricity of disappointment shooting back and forth between the lovely

Ukrainian and my kindly Personal Butler, the pity, really . . .

Sorry, uh, sorry for the, you know, trouble . . . I say.

No, sir, the lovely Ukrainian says. We are sorry to make any difficulties for you.

Ha, I thought, God bless you, now *this* is service, this is freaking Seven-Star Service!

But over the next few hours, my bliss diminished. I was approached by the Lebanese Floor Butler, by several Mysterious Callers from Guest Services, all of whom, politely but edgily, informed me that it would be much appreciated if the balance of the payment could be made by me pronto. I kept explaining my situation (that darn bank!), they kept accepting my explanation, and then someone else would call, or come by, once again encouraging me to pay the remaining cash, if I didn't mind terribly, right away, as was proper.

So although the Burj is a wonder—a Themed evocation of a reality that has never existed, unless in somebody's hashish dream—a kind of externalized fantasy of affluence, if that fantasy were being had in real time by a very rich Hedonistic Giant with unlimited access to some kind of Exaggeration Drug, a Giant fond of bright, mismatched colors, rounded, huge, inexplicable structures, dancing fountains, and two-story-tall wall-lining aquariums—I couldn't enjoy any of it. Not the electronic curtains that reveal infinite ocean; not the free-high-speed-Internet-accessing big-screen TV; not the Burj-shaped box of complimentary gourmet dates; not the shower with its six different Rube Goldbergian nozzles arranged so that one can wash certain body parts without having to demean oneself via bending or squatting; not the complimentary three-hundred-dollar bottle of wine; not the sweeping Liberace stairs or the remote-control front-door opener; not the distant view of The Palm, Jumeirah, and/or the tiny inconsequential boats far below, full of little people who couldn't afford to stay in the Burj even in their wildest dreams, the schmucks (although by the time of my third Admonitory Phone Call, I was feeling envious of them and their little completely paid-for boats, out there wearing shorts, shorts with, possibly, some cash in the pockets)—couldn't enjoy any of it, because I was too cowed to leave my room. I resisted the urge to crawl under the bed. I experienced a sudden fear that a group of Disapproving Guest Services People would appear at my remote-controlled door and physically escort me down to the lobby ATM (an ATM about which I expect I'll be having anxiety nightmares the rest of my life), which would once again prominently display the words PROVIDER DECLINES TRANSACTION. It's true what the Buddhists say: Mind can convert Heaven into Hell. This was happening to me. A headline in one of the nine complimentary newspapers read, actually read: "American Jailed for Nonpayment of Hotel Bill."

Perhaps someone had put acid in the complimentary Evian?

MON PETIT PATHETIC REBELLION

On one of my many unsuccessful missions to the ATM, I met an Indian couple from the United Kingdom who had saved up their money for this Dubai trip and were staying downtown, near the souk. They had paid fifty dollars to come in and have a look around the Burj (although whom they paid wasn't clear—the Burj says it discontinued its policy of charging for this privilege), and were regretting having paid this money while simultaneously trying to justify it. Although we must remember, said the husband to the wife, this is, after all, a once-in-a-lifetime experience! Yes, yes, of course, she said, I don't regret it for a minute! But there is a look, a certain look, about the eyes, that means: Oh God, I am gut-sick with worry about money. And these intelligent, articulate people had that look. (As, I suspect, did I.) There wasn't, she said sadly, that much to see, really, was there? And one felt rather watched, didn't one, by the help? Was there a limit on how long they could stay? They had already toured the lobby twice, been out to the ocean-overlooking pool, and were sort of lingering, trying to get their fifty bucks' worth.

At this point, I was, I admit it, like anyone at someone else's financial mercy, a little angry at the Burj, which suddenly seemed like a rosewater-smelling museum run for, and by, wealthy oppressors-of-the-people, shills for the new global economy, membership in which requires the presence of A Wad, and your ability to get to it/prove it exists.

Would you like to see my suite? I asked the couple.

Will there be a problem with the, ah . . .

Butler? I said. Personal Butler?

With the Personal Butler? he said.

Well, I am a guest, after all, I said. And you are, after all, my old friends from college in the States. Right? Could we say that?

We said that. I snuck them up to my room, past the Personal Butler, and gave them my complimentary box of dates and the three-hundred-dollar bottle of wine. Fight the power! Then we all stood around, feeling that odd sense of shame/solidarity that people of limited means feel when their limitedness has somehow been underscored.

Later that night, a little drunk in a scurvy bar in another hotel (described by L, my friend from Detroit, as the place where "Arabs with a thing for brown sugar" go to procure "the most exquisite African girls on the planet," but which was actually full of African girls who, like all girls whose job it is to fuck anyone who asks them night after night, were weary and joyless and seemed on the brink of tears), I scrawled in my notebook: *Paucity (ATM) = Rage.*

Then I imagined a whole world of people toiling in the shadow of approaching ruin, exhausting their strength and grace, while above them a whole other world of people puttered around, enjoying the good things of life, staying at the Burj just because they could.

And I left my ATM woes out of it and just wrote: *Paucity = Rage.*

LUCKILY, IT DIDN'T COME TO JAIL

Turns out, the ATM definition of "daily" is: after midnight in the United States. In the morning, as I marched the twenty-five hundred dirhams I owed proudly upstairs, the cloud lifted. A citizen of the affluent world again, I went openly to have coffee in the miraculous lobby, where my waiter and I talked of many things—of previous guests (Bill Clinton, 50 Cent—a "loud-laughing man, having many energetic friends"), and a current guest, supermodel Naomi Campbell.

Then I left the Burj, no hard feelings, and went somewhere even better, and more expensive.

HEAVEN FOR REAL, PLUS IN THIS
CASE IT WAS PAID FOR
IN ADVANCE

The Al Maha resort is located inside a stunningly beauti-ful/bleak, rugged desert nature preserve an hour outside of Dubai. My Personal Butler was possibly the nicest man I've ever met, who proudly admitted it was he who designed the linens, as well as the special Kleenex dispensers. He had been at Al Maha since the beginning. He loved it here. This place was his life's work.

Each villa had its own private pool.

After check-in, we're given a Jeep tour of the desert by a friendly and intensely knowledgeable South African guide, of that distinct subspecies of large, handsome guys who love nature. I learn things. The oryx at Al Maha have adapted to the new water-sprinkler system in the follow-ing way: at dusk, rather than going down to the spring, they sit at the base of the trees, waiting for the system to engage. I see a bush called Spine of Christ; it was from one of these, some believe, that Christ's crown of thorns was made. I see camel bones, three types of gazelle. We pass a concrete hut the size of a one-car garage, in a spot so isolated and desolate you expect some Beckett charac-ters to be sitting there. Who lives inside? A guy hired by the camel farmer, our guide says. He stays there day and night for months at a time. Who is he? Probably a Paki-stani; often, these camel-feeding outposts are manned by former child camel-jockeys, sold by their families to sheiks when the kids were four or five years old.

For lunch, we have a killer buffet, with a chef's spe-cial of veal medallions.

I go back to my villa for a swim. Birds come down to drink from my private pool. As you lower yourself into the pool, water laps forward and out, into a holding rim, then down into the Lawrencian desert. You see a plane of blue water, then a plane of tan desert. Yellow bees— completely yellow, as if spray-painted—flit around on the surface of the water.

At dusk we ride camels out into the desert. A truck meets us with champagne and strawberries. We sit on a dune, sipping champagne, watching the sunset. Dorkily, I am the only single. Luckily, I am befriended by B and K, a beautiful, affluent Dubai-Indian couple right out of Hemingway. She is pretty and loopy: Angelina Jolie meets Lucille Ball. He is elegant, reserved, kind-eyed, always admiring her from a little ways off, then rushing over to get her something she needs. They are here for their one-and-a-half-year anniversary. Theirs was a big traditional Indian wedding, held in a tent in the desert, attended by four hundred guests, who were transported in buses. In a traditional Indian wedding, the groom is supposed to enter on a white horse. White horses being in short supply in Dubai, her grandfather, a scion of old Dubai, called in a favor from a sheik, who flew in, from India, a beautiful white stallion. Her father then surprised the newlyweds with a thirty-minute fireworks show.

Fireworks, wow, I say, thinking of my wedding and our big surprise, which was, someone had strung a crap-load of Bud cans to the bumper of our rented Taurus.

She is her father's most precious possession, he says.

Does her father like you? I say.

He has no choice, he says.

Back at my room, out of my private pool, comes the

crazed Arabian moon, which has never, in my experience, looked more like a Ball of Rock in Space.

My cup runneth over. All irony vanishes. I am so happy to be alive. I am convinced of the essential goodness of the universe. I wish everyone I've ever loved could be here with me, in my private pool.

I wish *everyone* could be here with me, in my private pool: the blue-suited South Indians back in town, the camel farmer in his little stone box, the scared sad Moldavian prostitutes clutching their ostensibly sexy little purses at the Cyclone Club—I wish they could all, before they die, have one night at Al Maha.

But they can't.

Because that's not the way the world works.

"DUBAI IS WHAT IT IS BECAUSE ALL THE COUNTRIES AROUND IT ARE SO FUCKED UP"

In the middle of a harsh, repressive, backward, religiously excessive, physically terrifying region, sits Dubai. Its neighbors across the Gulf, Iraq and Iran, are war-torn and fanatic-ruled, respectively. Surrounding it is Saudi Arabia, where stealing will get your hand cut off, a repressive terrorist breeding ground where women's faces can't be seen in public, a country, my oil-industry friend says, on the brink of serious trouble.

The most worrisome thing in Saudi, he says, is the rural lower class. The urban middle class is doing all right, relatively affluent and satisfied. But look at a map of Saudi, he says: All that apparently empty space is not really empty. There are people there who are not middle-class and not happy. I say the Middle East seems something like Russia circa 1900—it's about trying to stave off revolution in a place where great wealth has been withheld from the masses by a greedy ruling class.

That's one way of saying it, he says.

Then he tells me how you get a date if you are a teenage girl in Saudi Arabia:

Go to the mall, wearing your required abaya. When a group of young guys walks by, if you see one you like, quickly find a secluded corner of the mall, take out your cell phone, lift your abaya, snap a picture of your face. Write your cell number on a piece of paper. When the boys walk by, drop the scrap at the feet of the one you like. When he calls, send him your photo. If he likes the photo, he will call again. Arrange a secret meeting.

The world must be peopled.

THE TRUTH IS, I CAN'T DECIDE WHAT'S TRUE, HONESTLY

One night, at dinner with some People Who Know, I blurt out a question that's been bothering me: Why doesn't Al Qaeda bomb Dubai, since Dubai represents/ tolerates decadent Western materialism, etc., and they could do it so easily? The Man Who Knows says, I'll tell you why: Dubai is like Switzerland during World War II—a place needed by everyone. The Swiss held Nazi money, Italian Fascist money. And in Dubai, according to this Person, Al Qaeda has millions of dollars in independent, Dubai-based banks, which don't always adhere to the international banking regulations that would require a bank to document the source of the income. A Woman Who Knows says she's seen it: A guy walks into a bank with a shitload of money, and they just take it, credit it, end of story. In this way, the People Who Know say, Dubai serves various illicit organizations from around the world: the Italian Mafia, the Spanish Mafia, etc., etc. Is this known about and blessed from the top down? Yes, it is. Al Qaeda needs Dubai, and Dubai tolerates Al Qaeda, making the periodic token arrest to keep the United States happy.

Later, the People Who Know are contradicted, in an elevator, by another Man Who Knows, a suave Luxembourgian who sells financial-services products to Dubai banks. Dubai has greatly improved its banking procedures since 9/11. Why would a terrorist group want to bank here? he asks. Think about it logically: Would they not be better served in a country sympathetic to them? Iran, Syria, Lebanon?

Good point, I say, thanking God in my heart that I am not a real Investigative Journalist.

IN WHICH SNOW IS MADE
BY A KENYAN

Arabian Ice City is part of a larger, months-long festival called Dubai Summer Surprises, which takes place at a dozen venues around town and includes Funny Magic Mirrors, Snow Magician Show, Magic Academy Workshop, Magic Bubble Show, Balloon Man Show, and Ice Cave Workshop, not to mention Ice Fun Character Show.

But Arabian Ice City is the jewel.

Because at Arabian Ice City, Arab kids see snow for the first time.

Arabian Ice City consists, physically, of: wall-length murals of stylized Swiss landscapes; two cardboard igloos labeled GENTS' MOSQUE and LADIES' MOSQUE, respectively (actual mosques, with shoes piled up inside the mock-ice doorways, through which people keep disappearing to pray); a huge ice cliff, which, on closer inspection, is a huge Styrofoam-like cliff, being sculpted frantically to look more like ice by twenty Filipinos with steak knives; and a tremendous central cardboard castle, inside of which, it is rumored, will be the Snow.

This is a local event, attended almost exclusively by Emiratis, sponsored by the local utility company; an opportunity, a representative tells me, to teach children about water and power conservation via educational activities and "some encouraging gifts." He's a stern, handsome, imposing presence, wearing, like every man in here but me, the full dishdasha. Has he been to America? He makes a kind of scoffing sound, as in: Right, pal, I'm going to America.

"America does not like Arabs," he says. "They think we are . . . I will not even say the word."

"Terrorists," I say.

He shuts his eyes in offended agreement.

Then he has to go. There is continued concern about the safety of the Arabian Ice City. Yesterday, at the opening, they expected one hundred people in the first hour, and instead got three thousand. Soon the ice was melting, the children, who knew nothing of the hazards of Snow, were slipping, getting hurt, and they'd had to shut the whole thing down, to much disappointment.

Waiting in the rapidly growing line, I detect a sense of mounting communal worry, fierce concern. This is, after all, for the children. Men rush in and out of the Ice Palace, bearing pillows, shovels, clipboards. Several Characters arrive and are ushered inside: a red crescent with legs; what looks like a drop of toothpaste, or, more honestly, sperm, with horizontal blue stripes; the crankiest-looking goose imaginable, with a face like a velociraptor and a strangely solicitous Sri Lankan handler, who keeps affectionately swatting the goose-raptor's tail and whispering things to it and steering it away from the crowd so they can have a private talk. The handler seems, actually, a little in love with the goose. As the goose approaches, a doorman announces, robustly, "Give a way for the goose!" The goose and goose-tender rush past, the tender swatting in lusty wonderment at the goose's thick tail, as if amazed that he is so privileged to be allowed to freely swat at such a thick, realistic tail.

The door opens, and in we go.

Inside is a rectangle about the size of a tennis court, green-bordered, like one of the ice rinks Sears used to sell. Inside is basically a shitload of crushed ice and one Kenyan with a shovel, madly crushing. And it does look like snow, kind of, or at least ice; it looks, actually, like a Syracuse parking lot after a freezing night.

Then the Arab kids pour in: sweet, proud, scared, tentative, trying to be brave. Each is offered a coat, from a big pile of identical coats, black with a red racing stripe. Some stand outside the snow rink, watching. Some walk stiff-legged across it, beaming. For others the approach is: Bend down, touch with one finger. One affects nonchalance: Snow is nothing to him. But then he quickly stoops, palms the snow, yanks his hand back, grins to himself. Another boy makes a clunky snowball, hands it politely to the crescent-with-legs, who politely takes it, holds it awhile, discreetly drops it. The goose paces angrily around the room, as if trying to escape the handler, who is still swatting flirtatiously at its tail while constantly whispering asides up at its beak.

And the kids keep coming. On their faces: looks of

bliss, the kind of look a person gets when he realizes he is in the midst of doing something rare, that might never be repeated, and is therefore of great value. They are seeing something from a world far away, where they will probably never go.

Women in abayas video. Families pose shyly, rearranging themselves to get more Snow in the frame. Mothers and fathers stand beaming at their kids, who are beaming at the Snow.

This is sweet, I scribble in my notebook.

And it is. My eyes well up with tears.

In the same way that reading the Bible, or listening to radio preachers, would not clue the neophyte in to the very active kindness of a true Christian home, reading the Koran, hearing about "moderate Islam," tells us nothing about the astonishing core warmth and familial sense of these Arab families.

I think: If everybody in America could see this, our foreign policy would change.

For my part, in the future, when I hear "Arab" or "Arab street" or those who "harbor, shelter, and sponsor" the terrorists, I am going to think of the Arabian Ice City, and that goose, moving among the cold-humbled kids, and the hundreds of videotapes now scattered around Arab homes in Dubai, showing beloved children reaching down to touch Snow.

WHAT IS JED CLAMPETT DOING
IN GITMO?

Having a Coke after Arabian Ice City, trying to get my crying situation sorted out, it occurred to me that the American sense of sophistication/irony—our cleverness, our glibness, our rapid-fire delivery, our rejection of gentility, our denial of tradition, our blunt realism—which can be a form of greatness when it manifests in a Gershwin, an Ellington, a Jackson Pollock—also causes us to (wrongly) assume a corresponding level of sophistication/irony/worldliness in the people of other nations.

Example One: I once spent some time with the mujahideen in Peshawar, Pakistan—the men who were at that time fighting the Russians and formed the core of the Taliban—big, scowling, bearded men who'd just walked across the Khyber Pass for a few weeks of rest. And the biggest, fiercest one of all asked me, in complete sincerity, to please convey a message to President Reagan, from him, and was kind of flabbergasted that I didn't know the president and couldn't just call him up for a chat, man-to-man.

Example Two: On the flight over to Dubai, the flight attendant announces that if we'd like to make a contribution to the Emirates Airline Foundation children's fund, we should do so in the provided envelope. The sickly Arab man next to me, whose teeth are rotten and who has, with some embarrassment, confessed to "a leg problem," responds by gently stuffing the envelope full of the sugar cookies he was about to eat. Then he pats the envelope, smiles to himself, folds his hands in his lap, goes off to sleep.

What one might be tempted to call simplicity could be more accurately called a limited sphere of experience. We round up "a suspected Taliban member" in Afghanistan and, assuming that Taliban means the same thing to him as it does to us (a mob of intransigent inconvertible Terrorists), whisk this sinister Taliban member—who grew up in, and has never once left, what is essentially the Appalachia of Afghanistan; who possibly joined the Taliban in response to the lawlessness of the post-Russian warlord state, in the name of bringing some order and morality to his life or in a misguided sense of religious fervor—off to Guantánamo, where he's treated as if he personally planned 9/11. Then this provincial, quite possibly not-guilty, certainly rube-like guy, whose view of the world is more limited than we can even imagine, is denied counsel and a possible release date, and subjected to all of the hardships and deprivations our modern military-prison system can muster. How must this look to him? How must we look to him?

My experience has been that the poor, simple people of the world admire us, are enamored of our boldness, are hopeful that the insanely positive values we espouse can be actualized in the world. They are, in other words, rooting for us. Which means that when we disappoint them—when we come in too big, kill innocents, when our powers of discernment are diminished by our frenzied, self-protective, fearful post-9/11 energy—we have the potential to disappoint them bitterly and drive them away.

LOOK, DREAM, BUT STAY OUT THERE

My fourth and final hotel, the Emirates Towers, is grand and imperial, surrounded by gardens, palm trees, and an elaborate fountain/moat assembly that would look right at home on an outlying *Star Wars* planet.

One Thai prostitute I spoke with in a bar said she'd stayed at the Emirates Towers four or five times but didn't like it much. Why not? I wondered. Too business-oriented? Kind of formal, a bit stuffy? "Because every time, they come up in the night and t'row me out," she said.

Returning to the hotel at dusk, I find dozens of the low-level South Indian workers, on their weekly half-day off, making their way toward the Towers, like peasants to the gates of the castle, dressed in their finest clothes (cowboy-type shirts buttoned to the throat), holding clunky circa-1980s cameras.

What are they doing here? I ask. What's going on?

We are on holiday, one says.

What are their jobs? When can they go home? What will they do tonight? Go out and meet girls? Do they have girlfriends back home, wives?

Maybe someday, one guy says, smiling a smile of anticipatory domestic ecstasy, and what he means is: Sir, if you please, how can I marry when I have nothing? This is why I'm here: so someday I can have a family.

Are you going in there? I ask, meaning the hotel.

An awkward silence follows. In there? Them?

No, sir, one says. We are just wishing to take photos of ourselves in this beautiful place.

They go off. I watch them merrily photographing themselves in front of the futuristic fountain, in the groves of lush trees, photos they'll send home to Hyder-abad, Bangalore. Entering the hotel is out of the ques-tion. They know the rules.

I decide to go in but can't locate the pedestrian entrance. The idea, I come to understand, after fifteen minutes of high-attentiveness searching, is to discourage foot traffic. Anybody who belongs in there will drive in and valet park.

Finally I locate the entrance: an unmarked, concealed, marble staircase with wide, stately steps fifty feet across. Going up, I pass a lone Indian guy hand-squeegeeing the thirty-three (I count them) steps.

How long will this take you? I ask. All afternoon?

I think so, he says sweetly.

Part of me wants to offer to help. But that would be, of course, ridiculous, melodramatic. He washes these stairs every day. It's not my job to hand-wash stairs. It's his job to hand-wash stairs. My job is to observe him hand-washing the stairs, then go inside the air-conditioned lobby and order a cold beer and take notes about his stair-washing so I can go home and write about it, making more for writing about it than he'll make in many, many years of doing it.

And of course, somewhere in India is a guy who'd kill to do some stair-washing in Dubai. He hasn't worked in three years, any chance of marriage is rapidly fading. Does this stair washer have any inclination to return to India, surrender his job to this other guy, give up his hard-won lifestyle to help this fellow human being? Who knows? If he's like me, he probably does. But in the end, his answer, like mine, is: That would be ridiculous, melodramatic. It's not my job to give up my job, which I worked so hard these many years to get.

Am I not me? Is he not him?

He keeps washing. I jog up the stairs to the hotel. Two smiling Nepalese throw open the huge doors, greeting me warmly, and I go inside.

GOOD-BYE, DUBAI, I'LL LOVE YOU FOREVER

Emirates Airline features unlimited free movies, music, and video games, as well as Downward-Looking and Forward-Looking live closed-circuit TV. I toggle back and forth between the Downward-Looking Camera (there are the Zagros Mountains, along the Iraq-Iran border) and

Meet the Fockers. The mountains are green, rugged. The little dog is flushed down the toilet and comes out blue.

It's a big world, and I really like it.

In all things, we are the victims of The Misconception From Afar. There is the idea of a city, and the city itself, too great to be held in the mind. And it is in this gap (between the conceptual and the real) that aggression begins. No place works any different than any other place, really, beyond mere details. The universal human laws—need, love for the beloved, fear, hunger, periodic exaltation, the kindness that rises up naturally in the absence of hunger/fear/pain—are constant, predictable, reliable, universal, and are merely ornamented with the details of local culture. What a powerful thing to know: that one's own desires are mappable onto strangers; that what one finds in oneself will most certainly be found in The Other—perhaps muted, exaggerated, or distorted, yes, but there nonetheless, and thus a source of comfort.

Just before I doze off, I counsel myself grandiosely: Fuck concepts. Don't be afraid to be confused. Try to remain permanently confused. Anything is possible. Stay open, forever, so open it hurts, and then open up some more, until the day you die, world without end, amen.

THANK YOU, ESTHER FORBES

It began, like so many things in those days, with a nun.
Unlike the other nuns at St. Damian School, who, it
seemed, had been born nuns, Sister Lynette seemed to
have been born an adorable, sun-dappled Kansas girl
with an Audrey Hepburn smile, who was then kidnapped
by a band of older, plumper, meaner nuns who were trying to break her. I was a little in love with Sister Lynette,
with her dry wit and good-heartedness and the wisp of
hair that snuck out from under her wimple. I thought
of a convent as a place of terrific rigor, where prospec-
tive nuns were given access to esoteric knowledge, which
they were then to secretly disseminate among select students in Middle America, to save the culture. Hoping to
be so identified, I would linger in Sister Lynette's classroom after school (both of us covered in chalk dust, my
wool pants smelling like Distressed Sheep) as she told
me stories about her Kansas girlhood. I entertained rescue fantasies, in which Sister realized that the best way

for her to serve God was to quit the nuns, marry me, and start wearing jeans as we traveled around the country making antiwar speeches. Since I was only in third grade, these fantasies required a pre-fantasy, in which pacifist aliens placed me in a sort of Aging Apparatus.

One afternoon, Sister Lynette handed me a book: *Johnny Tremain*, by Esther Forbes. This is the story of an arrogant apprentice silversmith in Boston during the Revolutionary War, whose prospects are cut short by a tragic accident until he finds a new sense of purpose in the war. The cover was a picture of a young Johnny, looking a bit like Twiggy. On it there was a shiny gold medallion: the Newbery Medal.

It was an award-winner.

Sister Lynette had given me an award-winner.

I was soon carrying it around twenty-four hours a day, the Newbery Medal facing out, as if I, and not Esther Forbes, had written *Johnny Tremain*.

"I think you can handle this," Sister had said as she handed me the book (she'd checked it out of the library), but what I heard was: "Only you, George, in this entire moronic class, can handle this. There is a spark in you, and it is that spark that keeps me from fleeing back to Kansas."

I imagined the scene at the convent—everyone in nun gear, sitting around a TV that was somehow always tuned to *The Flying Nun*. And then Sister Lynette makes her announcement:

"I'm thinking of giving Saunders *Johnny Tremain*."

A tense silence.

"Isn't that . . . ," asks Sister Humiline, the principal, "an award-winner?"

"It is," says Sister Lynette. "But I think he's ready."

"Well, then . . . ," says Sister Humiline. Clearly this

is important. Denied this, Sister Lynette might make her break for Kansas. "Let him give it a try, then. But, truly, I wonder if he's got it in him. That book is hard, and he is only a third-grader."

"Even I had trouble with it," pipes up a junior nun.

"I think he can handle it," says Sister Lynette.

And the wonderful thing was: I could. I loved the language, which was dense and seemed not to care that it sounded mathematically efficient ("On rocky islands gulls woke"). The sentences somehow had got more life in them than normal sentences had. They were not merely sentences but compressed moments that burst when you read them. I often left the book open on the kitchen table, so that my mother and her friends could see how at home I was with phrases like "too cripple-handed for chopping open sea chests" or "Isannah drank herself sick and silly on sillabubs."

A sentence, Forbes seemed to believe, not only had to say something, it had to say it uniquely, with verve. A sentence was more than just a fact-conveyor; it also made a certain sound, and could have a thrilling quality of being over-full, saying more than its length should permit it to say. A sequence of such sentences exploding in the brain made the invented world almost unbearably real, each sentence serving as a kind of proof.

The tragic accident that happens early in the book ends Johnny's silversmithing: his right thumb is melded to the palm of his hand by molten silver. During recess, I started holding my hand like his in the pocket of my coat, trying to get through the entire period without uncrippling myself. There was a sweetness in the bitterness I felt as I imagined that I was Johnny and the whole world had turned against me, even my fiancée, Cilla, and her real-life corollary, Susan Pusateri. Had Susan smiled?

She would marry me in spite of my deformity. Was she talking energetically to Joey Cannarozzi? She preferred his fully opposable thumb, and I would therefore have to lay siege to the British armory.

After a while, because I liked the idea of being wounded, but didn't much like the idea of actually having that pink flipperlike thing flapping around on my arm, a world-famous surgeon from France would arrive in the Boston in my head and fix my hand, and I would go back to class, face chapped from the wind, holding the book in my now-perfect hand, Newbery Medal facing outward.

"Good book?" Sister Lynette would say from her desk.

"Good book," I would say.

Before *Johnny Tremain*, writers and writing gave me the creeps. In our English book, which had one of those 1970s titles that connoted nothing (*Issues and Perspectives*, maybe, or *Amalgam 109*), the sentences ("Larry, aged ten, a tow-headed heavyset boy with a happy smile for all, meandered down to the ballfield, hoping against hope he would at last be invited to join some good-spirited game instigated by the other lads of summer") repulsed me the way a certain kind of moccasin-style house slipper then in vogue among my father's friends repulsed me. I would never, I swore, wear slippers like that. Only old people who had given up on life could wear slippers like that. Likewise the sentences in *Amalgam 109* or *Polyglot Viewpoints* seemed to have given up on life, or to never have taken life sufficiently personally. They weren't lies, exactly, but they weren't true either. They lacked will. They seemed committee-written, seemed to emanate from no-person, to argue against the intimate actual feeling of minute-to-minute life.

Forbes suggested that the sentence was where the battle was fought. With enough attention, a sentence could peel away from its fellows and be, not only from you, but *you*. I later found the same quality in Hemingway, in Isaac Babel, Gertrude Stein, Henry Green: sentences that had been the subject of so much concentration, they had become things in the world instead of attempts to catalog it.

A person can write: "There were, out in the bay, a number of rocks, islands of a sort, and upon these miniature islands, there resided a number of gulls, which, as the sun began to rise, gradually came to life, ready to begin another day of searching for food."

Or she can write: "On rocky islands gulls woke."

The first sentence is perfectly correct. There is, strictly speaking, more information in it than in the second. But is the increased information justified by the greater number of words? The second sentence credits our intelligence. Where else would the islands be, but in a bay? The plural "islands" implies that there are "a number" of them. If the rocks are "islands of a sort," let's call them "islands." Gulls search for food every day, no need to point it out.

The second sentence has been loved by its creator. She has given it her full attention. That missing comma? She meant it. There was, to Forbes, I expect, a world of difference between, "On rocky islands, gulls woke," and "On rocky islands gulls woke."

Standing around the school yard, I tried out sentences meant to describe, with Forbes-like precision, whatever I happened to be seeing: "Sister Lynette was eating lunch in the doorway while watching the third- and fourth-grade kids running around in the parking lot at recess and as she watched them, she thought of her home in Kansas." That wasn't very Forbes-ish. Sister Lynette wasn't actually standing in the doorway at all. She was . . . she was "standing on the sidewalk that ran between the school building itself and the parking lot on which the children played." Or actually, she was "standing with one foot on that sidewalk and one foot in the parking lot." Did we need all that? Was her exact position worth the resulting sentence-bulk? Why did we care where she was standing anyway? Did it affect what came next? Also, she wasn't watching "the third- and fourth-grade kids." She was watching *some* of them. Actually, on closer inspection, she wasn't. She was looking across the street, at a run-down house. What did I mean by "run-down"? What were the specific characteristics of the house that might cause me to think of it as "run-down"?

I remember those times with great affection: the bitter Chicago cold, the vast parking lot, the world, suddenly and for the first time, transformed into something describable, with me, the Potential Describer, at its center.

The world, I started to see, was a different world, depending on what you said about it, and how you said it. By honing the sentences you used to describe the world, you changed the inflection of your mind, which changed your perceptions.

The difference between Esther Forbes and the authors of *Polyglot 141* was that Forbes had fully invested herself in her sentences. She had made them her own, agreed to live or die by them, taken total responsibility for them. How had she done this? I didn't know. But I do now: she'd revised them. She had abided long enough with each of them to push past the normal into what we might call the *excessive-meaningful*; had held the prose up to sufficient scrutiny to turn it into something iconic, something that sounded like her and only like her.

What happens when this attention is not paid?

Well, *Polyglot 141* happens.

But worse things can happen than *Polyglot 141*.

A petty bureaucrat writes to his superior: "The lighting must be better protected than now. Lights could be eliminated, since they apparently are never used. However, it has been observed that when the doors are shut, the load always presses hard against them as soon as darkness sets in. This is because the load naturally rushes toward the light when darkness sets in, which makes closing the door difficult. Also, because of the alarming nature of darkness, screaming always occurs when the doors are closed. It would therefore be useful to light the lamp before and during the first moments of the operation." The bureaucrat was the ironically named "Mr. Just," his organization the SS, the year 1942.

What Mr. Just did not write—what he would have written, had he been taking full responsibility for his own prose—is: "To more easily kill the Jews, leave the lights on." But writing this would have forced him to admit what he was up to. To avoid writing this, what did he have to do? Disown his prose. Pretend his prose was not him. He may have written a more honest version, and tore it up. He may have intuitively, self-protectively, skipped directly to this dishonest, passive-voice version. Either way, he accepted an inauthentic relation to his own prose, and thereby doomed himself to hell.

Working with language is a means by which we can identify the bullshit within ourselves (and others). If we learn what a truthful sentence looks like, a little flag goes up at a false one. False prose can mark an attempt to evade responsibility ("On structures not unlike rock masses, it was observed that certain animals perhaps prone to flight slept somewhat less aggressively than previously"), or something more diabolical ("The germ-ridden avatars of evil perched on their filthy black rocks in the otherwise pure bay, daring the clear-souled inhabitants of the city to do what was so obviously necessary: kill them before they could infest the city's hopeful, innocent children"); the process of improving our prose disciplines the mind, hones the logic, and, most important of all, tells us what we really think. But this process takes time, and immersion in prior models of beautiful compression.

Forbes was my first model of beautiful compression. She did for me what one writer can do for another: awoke a love for sentences. Behind her prose I sensed the loving hand of an involved human maker. Her thirst for direct, original language seemed like a religion of sorts, a method of orientation, and a comfort, in all countries and weathers, in happiness and sadness, in sickness and in health. Reading *Johnny Tremain*, I felt a premonition that immersion in language would enrich and bring purpose to my life, which has turned out to be true.

So thank you, Esther Forbes. I never knew you, it turned out your Boston never existed, but that nonexistent town, and that boy made out of words, changed things for me forever.

A SURVEY
OF THE
LITERATURE

The Patriotic Studies discipline may properly be said to have begun with the work of Jennison, et al., which first established the existence of the so-called "fluid-nations," entities functionally identical to the more traditional geographically based nations ("geo-nations"), save for their lack of what the authors termed "spatial/geographic continuity." Citizenship in a fluid-nation was seen to be contingent not upon residence in some shared physical space (i.e., within "borders") but, rather, upon commonly held "values, loyalties, and/or habitual patterns of behavior" seen to exist across geo-national borders.

For approximately the first five years of its existence, the Patriotic Studies discipline proceeded under the assumption that these fluid-nations were benign entities, whose existence threatened neither the stability nor integrity of the traditional geo-nation.

A classic study of this period was conducted by Emmons, Denny, and Smith, concerning the fluid-nation

Men Who Fish. Using statistical methods of retro-attribution, the authors were able to show that, in a time of national crisis (the Battle of the Bulge, Europe, 1944), American citizens who were also citizens of Men Who Fish performed their duties every bit as efficiently (± 5 Assessment Units) as did members of the control group, even when that duty involved inflicting "harm" to "serious harm" on fellow citizens of Men Who Fish who were allied at that time with the opposing geo-nation (i.e., Germany). During this battle, as many as seventy-five hundred (and no less than five thousand) German soldiers who were citizens of Men Who Fish were killed or wounded by American soldiers who were citizens of Men Who Fish, leading the authors to conclude that citizens of Men Who Fish were not "expected, in a time of national crisis, to respond significantly less patriotically than a control group of men of similar age, class, etc., who are not citizens of Men Who Fish."

Significant and populous fluid-nations examined during this so-called "Exoneration Studies" period included Men With Especially Large Penises; People Who Say They Hate Television But Admit To Watching It Now And Then, Just To Relax; Women Who When Drunk Berate The Sport Of Boxing; and Elderly Persons Whose First Thought Upon Hearing Of A Death Is Relief That They Are Still Alive, Followed By Guilt For Having Had That First Feeling.

A watershed moment in the history of the discipline occurred with the groundbreaking work of Randall, Cleary, et al., which demonstrated for the first time that individuals were capable of holding multiple fluid-nation citizenships. Using the newly developed Anders-Reese Distance-Observation Method, the authors were able to provide specific examples of this phenomenon.

A Nebraska man was seen to hold citizenship in both Men Who Sit Up Late At Night Staring With Love At Their Sleeping Children, and Farmers Who Mumble Soundless Prayers While Working In Their Fields. In Cincinnati, Ohio, twin sisters were found to belong to Five-Times-A-Week Churchgoers, as well as Clandestine Examiners Of One's Own Hardened Nasal Secretions. An entire family in Abilene, Texas, was seen to belong to Secretly Always Believe They Are The Ugliest In The Room, with individual members of this family also holding secondary citizenships in fluid-nations as diverse as Listens To Headphones In Bed; Stands Examining Her Breasts In Her Closet; Brags Endlessly While Actually Full of Doubt; Makes Excellent Strudel; and Believes Fervently In The Risen Christ.

At the time, awareness of our work among the general public was still low. This would change dramatically, however, with the publication, by Beatts, Daniels, and Ahkerbaj, of their comprehensive study of the fluid-nation People Reluctant To Kill For An Abstraction.

In this study, 155 members of the target fluid-nation were assessed per the Hanley-Briscombe National Allegiance Criterion, a statistical model developed to embody the Dooley-Sminks-Ang Patriot Descriptor Statement, which defined a patriot as "an individual who, once the leadership of his country has declared that action is necessary, responds quickly, efficiently, and without wasteful unnecessary questioning of the declared national goal."

Results indicated that citizens of People Reluctant To Kill For An Abstraction scored, on average, thirty-nine points lower on the National Allegiance Criterion than did members of the control group and exhibited nonpatriotic attitudes or tendencies 29 percent more

often. Shown photographs of members of an opposing geo-nation and asked, "What sort of person do you
believe this person to be?" citizens of People Reluctant
To Kill For An Abstraction were 64 percent more likely
to choose the response "Don't know, would have to meet
them first." Given the opportunity to poke with a rubber baton a citizen of a geo-nation traditionally opposed
to their geo-nation (an individual who was at that time
taunting them with a slogan from a list of Provocative
Slogans), citizens of People Reluctant To Kill For An
Abstraction were found to be 71 percent less likely to
poke than members of the control group.

The authors' conclusion ("It is perhaps not inaccurate to state that, within this particular fluid-nation, loyalty to the fluid-nation may at times surpass loyalty to
the parent geo-nation"), along with the respondent's pro-
fessed willingness to subjugate important geo-national
priorities, and even accept increased national security
risks, in order to avoid violating the Cohering Principle
of their fluid-nation (i.e., not killing for an abstraction),
led to the creation of a new category of fluid-nation, the
so-called Malignant fluid-nation.

At this time—coincidentally but fortuitously—there
appeared the work of Elliott, Danker, et al., who made
the important (and at the time startling) discovery that
multiple fluid-nation citizenships *did not occur in random distributions*. That is, given a known fluid-nation
citizenship, it was theoretically possible to predict an
individual's future citizenships in other fluid-nations,
using complex computer modeling schemes. The authors
found, for example, that citizens of Over-Involved Mothers tended to become, later in life, citizens of either
Over-Involved Grandmothers or (perhaps paradoxically)
Completely Disinterested Grandmothers, with high rates

of occurrence observed also in Women Who Collect Bird Statuary and Elderly Women Who Purposely Affect A "Quaint Old Lady" Voice.

The implications of these data vis-à-vis the so-called Malignant fluid-nations were clear. Work immediately began within the discipline to identify and develop innovative new technologies for the purpose of identifying those fluid-nations most likely to produce future citizens of Malignant fluid-nations. The most sophisticated and user-friendly of these tools proved to be the Rowley Query Grid, which successfully predicted the probability that citizens of Tends To Hold Him/Herself Aloof From The Group (previously thought to be Innocuous) would, in time, evolve into citizens of People Reluctant To Kill For An Abstraction. Subsequently, dozens of these Nascent-Malignant fluid-nations were identified, including Bilingual Environmentalists, Crusty Ranchers, Angry Widowers, and Recent Immigrants With An Excessive Interest In The Arts.

Needless to say, these findings resulted in dramatic improvement in both the National Security Index and the Unforeseen Violence Probability Statistic.

Entire research departments have now embarked on the herculean task of identifying all extant fluid-nations, with particular emphasis, of course, on links to known Malignant fluid-nations. The innovative work of Ralph Frank, in which fifty individuals waiting for a bus in Portland, Oregon, were, briefly and with their full consent, taken into custody and administered the standard Fluid-Nation Identifier Questionnaire, indicated the worrisome ubiquity of these fluid-nations. At least ninety-seven separate fluid-nations were detected within this random gathering of Americans, including: Now-Heavy Former Ballerinas; Gum-Chompers; People

Who Daydream Obsessively Of Rescuing Someone Famous; Children Of Mothers Who Were Constantly Bursting Into Tears; Men Who Can Name Entire Line-ups Of Ball Teams From Thirty Years Ago; Individuals In Doubt That Someone Will Ever Love Him/Her; and Individuals Who Once Worked, Or Considered Working, As Clowns. A closer analysis of the fluid-nations identified indicated that *nearly 50 percent of these* had been, would soon be, or very possibly could eventually be linked to People Reluctant To Kill For An Abstraction, or to another Malignant fluid-nation.

It is thus no longer a question of whether a large number of Americans belong to problematic fluid-nations; it is, rather, a question of how willing Americans are to freely confess these citizenships, and then undergo the necessary mitigative measures, so that the nation need have no doubt about their readiness to respond in an emergency.

One need only imagine the catastrophic results, should the American membership of one of the more ubiquitous fluid-nations (Parents Of Children Inclined To Cry During Thunderstorms, for example, or Insepa-rable Married Couples Who Whisper Together Late Into The Night) pause during some national crisis to con-sider the effects of the national protective action upon their fellow fluid-nation members who happened to be residing within the geo-nation which was at that time posing the threat to American security (i.e., the "enemy nation").

Although much work remains to be done, most Americans now recognize the tremendous danger posed by these fluid-nations, are energetically examining them-selves and their acquaintances for the residual pres-ence of any questionable loyalties or allegiances, and have come to recognize that national security issues are most efficiently addressed, not by the average citizen, who is (understandably) somewhat underinformed and distracted, but by the well-trained, highly skilled professionals working within the Patriotic Studies discipline.

This is not, of course, just an American issue; leaders of other geo-nations have now begun to recognize the potential gravity of this threat. Throughout the world, at any given moment, the justifiable aims of legitimate geo-nations are being threatened by reckless individuals who insist on indulging their private, inscrutable agendas. The prospect of a world plagued by these fluid-nations—a world in which one's identification with, and loyalty to, one's parent geo-nation is constantly being undermined—is sobering indeed. This state of affairs would not only allow for, but require, a constant, round-the-clock reassessment of one's values and beliefs prior to action, a continual adjustment of one's loyalties and priorities based on an ongoing evaluation and reevaluation of reality—a process that promises to be as inefficient as it is wearying.

The above summary has, of necessity, been brief. It will be left to future scholars, working in a time of relative calm, once the present national crisis has receded, to tell the full story, in all the rich detail it deserves.

MR. VONNEGUT
IN SUMATRA

At twenty-three, recent engineering grad that I was, I had read virtually nothing. But there was hope: I was living four out of every six weeks in the Sumatran jungle. On leave in Singapore, I loaded up on books to take back to the seismic crew. This was serious business. If the books ran out before the four weeks did, I would be reduced to reading the same 1979 *Playboy* over and over, and/or watching hours of *wayang* theater on the bunkhouse television. Occasionally one of our contractors would bring porn, which often involved animals. We were obliged to watch and be grateful, then discuss the details of certain scenes with him. This contractor had once locked a fever-struck employee in a shed, where he died. This contractor was supposedly magically protected from all attacks on his person. He had so far survived three shootings and a hatchet attack, which was why, wittily, he was called Hatchet.

I was, to understate the case, an untrained reader.

My understanding of literature at this time was: great writing was hard reading. What made something great was you could barely understand it. A scene I'd been imagining as taking place indoors would suddenly sprout stars and a riverfront. At a fictional dinner party at which I'd understood there to be three people present, six were suddenly required, based on the appearance of three unfamiliar names. In addition to the difficulties posed by my dullness, I also selected books oddly. The writers I preferred were writers whose English was least like mine. I believed great writing was done in a language that had as little as possible to do with the one I spoke. The words were similar but arranged more cleverly, less directly. A good literary sentence was like a floor with a hole hidden in it. You dropped into the basement and, scratching your head, thought: "Why'd he say it that way? He must really be a great writer." Plain American language was like the pale ineffectual relative you took for granted: always there, a little embarrassing. Plain American was fine for getting around your dopey miniature world, cashing checks and finding restaurants and talking about television and so on, but when the real work of Art was required, you hauled out the fancy language, the one nobody used. I had started writing a little by this time, sneaking back into the office after-hours to produce such early, Asia-centric masterpieces as "Be Not Afraid in Thy Deep Monotheistic Veritable Heart of the Jungle" and "Black River That Runs Through Various Metaphorical Villages." Writing was, at this stage in my development, the process of trying to do whatever was most unnatural. Art was that thing you couldn't quite reach. The hope was that someday, when enough failure had been logged, a miracle would happen, and one would briefly be launched above one's station, suddenly able to write in that impossible, inscrutable, nineteenth-century language of the masters, and this miracle would happen often enough that one could eventually cobble together the two hundred or so pages it took to make a Real Book.

Then, on one of my Singapore jaunts, I picked up Kurt Vonnegut's *Slaughterhouse Five*. I knew, vaguely, that this was a classic. I knew it had to do with World War II, that the author had been present at the firebombing of Dresden. This sounded promising. At this time I also believed, courtesy of my hero Ernest Hemingway, that great writing required a Terrible Event One Had Witnessed. With any luck, one had been wounded during the Terrible Event, although not too badly. If not a physical wound, a mental wound was fine. The Terrible Event was what I was in Asia seeking. I had been to the Cambodian border seeking it, been to the Khyber Pass seeking it, but everywhere I went, was too cautious to be blown up or see anything horrific. Given the chance to get into real danger, I would think: *Jeez, that sounds dangerous,* retreat to my reasonably priced hotel, and read Hemingway.

But here was Vonnegut, a guy who had witnessed one of the most Terrible Events of his time. I was excited to see what he'd done with it. I hoped he hadn't wasted it. I hoped he'd done something like Hem had done with it. I hoped he had come out of it sobered and sullen, broken by his Terrible Event, but also that he had taken notes, so his book would be filled with pages of terse literary descriptions that showed that, though wounded, he still appreciated a good sunbeam slanting across a crude wooden table or a nice wind-ruffled stand of oak trees through which a river flowed pleasantly.

But then I started reading. In chapter one, right

off the bat, Vonnegut admits to trying and failing, over many years, to write the very book I was looking forward to reading: "As a trafficker in climaxes and thrills and characterization and wonderful dialogue and suspense and confrontations," he writes, "I had outlined the Dresden story many times." But then he admits: "I don't think this book . . . is ever going to be finished. I must have written five thousand pages by now, and thrown them all away." In chapter one he seems determined not to tell his war story at all. He writes, conversationally, about his days as a reporter, relates an anecdote about a visit with an old war buddy; scrolls through histories of the Crusades and of Dresden; quotes Roethke, Erika Ostrovsky, and the Gideon Bible; describes the carp in the Hudson River ("big as atomic submarines"). Then he offers this advance apology for the book we're reading: "It is so short and jangled . . . because there is nothing intelligent to say about a massacre." It's an introductory chapter, one the reader suspects was written last, when the rest of the book was already finished, but still, the effect is of a haunted man, delaying for as long as possible telling the big, sad story he's been trying to get off his chest for years, realizing that if he insists on telling it in a grand style, it may get told falsely, or never be told at all.

In chapter two the story finally began. But immediately there were more avoidances of the lyric/epic masterpiece I longed to be reading. Because suddenly, here came some space aliens, from Trafalmadore, "two feet high, and green, and shaped like plumber's friends." *What the heck?* I was thinking, back in Sumatra, in 1982, *this is a classic?* Aliens did not belong in classics. Aliens belonged in movies. Aliens were great; I loved aliens in movies, but I did not want them in my Literature. What I wanted in my Literature was a somber, wounded, masterly presence, regarding the world with a jaundiced, totally humorless eye.

But no, Vonnegut was funny. Funny? Hem wasn't funny. Only people I knew, like my beloved father and uncles, were funny. How wounded could he be, if he was so funny? The book was loose, episodic, written in the vernacular. This guy who had been in the belly of the beast wrote as if he were still, like me, a regular person from the Midwest. He wrote as if there were a continuum of consciousness between himself before and after his Terrible Event. Vonnegut did not seem to be saying, as I understood Hem to be saying, that his Terrible Event had forever exempted him from the usual human obligations of being kind, attempting to understand, behaving decently. On the contrary, Vonnegut seemed to feel that unkindness—a simple, idiotic failure of belief in the human, by men and their systems—had been the *cause* of his Terrible Event, and that what he had learned from this experience was not the importance of being tough and hard and untouchable, but the importance of preserving the kindness in ourselves at all costs.

There we were, in the deep German woods, behind enemy lines, but there was very little tension and almost no physical description. Vonnegut was skipping the lush physical details he had presumably put himself into so much danger to obtain. He was assuming these physical details; that is, he was assuming that I was supplying them. A forest was a forest, he seemed to be saying, let's not get all flaky about it. He did not seem to believe, as I had read Tolstoy did, that his purpose as a writer was to use words to replicate his experience, to make you feel and think and see what he had felt. This book was not a recounting of Vonnegut's actual war experience, but a *usage* of it. What intrigued me—also annoyed me—was trying to figure out the *purpose* of this usage. If he wasn't trying to make me know what he knew and feel what he'd felt, then what was the book *for*?

I'd understood the function of art to be primarily *descriptive*: a book was a kind of scale model of life, intended to make the reader feel and hear and taste and think just what the writer had. Now I began to understand art as a kind of black box the reader enters. He enters in one state of mind and exits in another. The writer gets no points just because what's inside the box bears some linear resemblance to "real life"—he can put whatever he wants in there. What's important is that something undeniable and nontrivial happens to the reader between entry and exit.

Your real story may have nothing to do with your actual experience, Vonnegut seemed to be saying. In constructing your black box, feel free to shorthand those experiences, allude to them sideways, or omit them entirely. Joke about them, avoid directly exploiting them, shroud them in an over-story about aliens: you know what you know, and that knowledge will not be shaken out of your stories no matter how breezy or comic or minimalist your mode of expression, or how much you shun mimesis.

I began to see, for example, that my knowledge of Hatchet—his casual cruelty, his unquestioning belief in his own right to run roughshod over others—could be used in fiction without needing to get bogged down in the burden of representing Hatchet in slavishly realistic terms. I could riff on Hatchet, instill his mind-set in a totally invented character (a space alien, a duck, a talking paper clip), could, in other words, use that portion of my mind labeled "Hatchet knowledge" in any way I saw fit. Hatchet's existence staked out a certain ontological space (*cruelty is real*, say), and the fact that I had known him gave me the right to use this cruelty-awareness in a story, even disassociated from his person.

In fact, *Slaughterhouse Five* seemed to be saying, our most profound experiences may *require* this artistic uncoupling from the actual. The black box is meant to change us. If the change will be greater via the use of invented, absurd material, so be it. We are meant to exit the book altered.

As for the exact nature of the alteration, Vonnegut's goal seemed to be to soften the heart, to encourage our capacity for pity and sorrow. Whatever would most soften the heart, is what belonged in the book. The sci-fi elements could be understood as a form of dramatic compression, meant to urge us more directly toward the truth of our existence: Do we travel in time? We do. Are there aliens that see us and judge us? There are, although they are in our heads, and sometimes we call them "Gods," or "our conscience," or "the superego."

I'd like to say I found all of this liberating but at the time I didn't. I couldn't stop reading the book, went back and read it again—but in the way earnest young idiots have, I was anxious to discount it. Why? The aliens, the aversion to conventional drama, the jokes, the humility of the book, scared me. I was, then even more than now, a control freak, and the book felt like an ode to the abandonment of control, a disavowal of mastery. The young, Ayn Randish Republican that I was, discounted Vonnegut as one of *them*: A former hippie, maybe, or proto-hippie, someone who, unlike me, wasn't earnest/tough/focused enough to be huge, classic, and utterly pure.

It would be years before I grasped the real power and beauty of the book, but a seed had been planted, and whenever I wrote or read something phony-baloney, there in the back of my mind was the Vonnegut of *Slaughter-house Five*, looking askance at that false thing, waiting for me to see the falseness of it too.

Humor is what happens when we're told the truth quicker and more directly than we're used to. The comic is the truth stripped of the habitual, the cushioning, the easy consolation. An "auditorium filled with two thousand men and women eagerly awaiting a night's entertainment" could also correctly be described as "two thousand smiling future moldering corpses" or "a mob of bodies that, only hours earlier, had, during the predressing phase, been standing scattered around town, in their underwear."

This rapid-truthing is what Vonnegut does with the war. He takes an unusual vector through it. He refuses the usual conceptual packaging we associate with "war" and "soldiers" and "battles" and "prisoners of war." "Soldier" is taken apart with a sad, sharp eye: "Billy was wearing a thin field jacket, a shirt and trousers of scratchy wool, and long underwear that was soaked with sweat. He was the only one of the four who had a beard. It was a random, bristly beard, and some of the bristles were white, even though Billy was only twenty-one years old. He was also going bald. Wind and cold and violent exercise had turned his face crimson. He didn't look like a soldier at all. He looked like a filthy flamingo." Even the German soldiers are mere guys in uniforms. Even the German attack dog is real and pathetic (cowering, stolen from a farmer, named Princess).

At the heart of Vonnegut's voice is a humility my earnest young self didn't feel comfortable with: In it, I heard evidence of real humiliation. War really was hell, with hell being the place where whatever you normally counted on or leaned on was taken from you, absolutely. Billy Pilgrim is a skinny virginal dork, and when he gets to war, war leaps on his skinny dorkitude and devastates him unglamorously, and haunts him ever after. Wild Bob is just some guy from Wyoming who gets all forty-five hundred of his men killed, then dies insane in a boxcar. Roland Weary, a Hemingway stand-in, all self-control and stealth, ends up trudging along on feet bloodied from the little boy's clogs he's forced to wear, sobbingly begging Pilgrim to "Walk right! Walk right!"

Vonnegut seemed to have been in a place where all the comforting verities had been stripped away, and was now cautiously trying to reconstruct a meaningful language out of what scraps of certainty he had left. Better to say too little, he seemed to feel, than too much, if, in saying too much, you might say something false. He'd been rendered a minimalist by aversion to bullshit and, if anything, was more of a purist than Hemingway in this regard.

Early in the book, Vonnegut is confronted by Mary, the angry wife of his old war buddy, Bernard V. O'Hare. She knows the kind of war novel he's going to write. "You'll pretend you were men instead of babies," she says, "and you'll be played in the movies by Frank Sinatra and John Wayne or some of those other glamorous, war-loving, dirty old men. And war will look just wonderful, so we'll have a lot more of them. And they'll be fought by babies like the babies upstairs."

He makes her a promise: in the movie of his book, there won't be a part for Frank Sinatra or John Wayne. In fact, he'll call his book *The Children's Crusade*. It will be, really be, an antiwar book.

And it is.

It didn't, of course, stop any wars. As Vonnegut reminds us early on, war will not be stopped. When a director friend asks if his book is an antiwar book, Vonnegut replies that he guesses it is.

"You know what I say to people when I hear they're writing antiwar books?" the friend says. "'Why don't you write an anti*glacier* book instead?'"

No, war will not be stopped. But it is a comfort, in the midst of a war, to read an antiwar book this good, and be reminded that just because something keeps happening, doesn't mean we get to stop regretting it. Massacres are bad, the death of innocents is bad, hate is bad, and there's something cleansing about hearing it said so purely.

What good the prophet in the wilderness may do is incremental and personal. It's good for us to hear someone speak the irrational truth. It's good for us when, in spite of all of the sober, pragmatic, and even correct arguments that war is sometimes necessary, someone says: war is large-scale murder, us at our worst, the stupidest guy doing the cruelest thing to the weakest being.

It's not as if the world will ever live by the extreme truth this prophet is speaking. War will never vanish from the face of the earth. Neither will sickness, but it's good to hear someone praising the blessing of health.

Earlier today, almost forty years after it was written, and in the middle of another war, I sat in my kitchen reading *Slaughterhouse Five*. The book didn't stop the current war, and won't stop the next one, or the one after that. But something in me rose to the truth in it, and I was put in proper relation to the war going on now. I was, if you will, forbidden to misunderstand it. It is what it is: massacre and screaming and confusion and blood and death. It is the mammoth projection outward of the confused inner life of a handful of men. When someone says war is inevitable, or unavoidable, or unfortunate but necessary, they may be right. Vonnegut's war was necessary. And yet it was massacre and screaming and confusion and blood and death. It was the mammoth projection outward of the confused inner life of men. In war, the sad tidy constructs we make to help us believe life is orderly and controllable are roughly thrown aside like the delusions they are. In war, love is outed as an insane, insupportable emotion, a kind of luxury emotion, because everywhere you look, someone beloved to someone is being slaughtered, by someone whose own beloved has been slaughtered, or will be, or could be.

There's something sacred about reading a book like *Slaughterhouse Five*, even if nothing changes but what's going on inside our minds. We leave such a book restored, if only briefly, to a proper relation with the truth, reminded of what is what, temporarily undeluded, our better nature set back on its feet.

A BRIEF STUDY OF THE BRITISH

STATEMENT OF PURPOSE

I had heard about the British all my life. As a child, I had crushes on a series of Britons, including Hayley Mills, Julie Andrews, and, somewhat problematically, Davy Jones. But for various reasons, including working for a living and not having enough money, I had never been to Britain.

It is my belief that we Americans, geographically isolated as we are, tend to be perhaps not as knowledgeable about other cultures as we might be. This is regrettable. Since we are the sole remaining superpower, it is desirable that we know something about the rest of the world, because otherwise, when we take over different parts of the world, how will we know how good we did?

Accordingly, I decided to undertake a visit to Britain, and study the land and its peoples.

A WORD ABOUT NOMENCLATURE

Britain is often said to be part of "the United Kingdom," along with several other countries, including England. Ireland is also nearby, and is considered part of Scotland, which, in turn, is adjacent to, and included in, a small country called Wales. To first-time visitors, this can be confusing, especially when one learns that— paradoxically—France is considered by the British to be its very own nation! One finds oneself longing for the simplicity of America, where, for example, everyone understands that New York City is a city, that Cleveland is a state in either Ohio or Indiana, and that the Mississippi River, I'm pretty sure, does not run in any other state than Mississippi. Or city. I can't remember if Mississippi is a city or a—anyway, the point is, the American visitor to Britain can avoid all confusion by simply referring to his hosts and hostesses as "you guys."

UP, UP, AND AWAY!

To get to Britain, you fly over several oceans, including the Atlantic. I think also Missouri? I did not see very much of the Atlantic or Missouri or whatever because, as we passed over, I was watching a movie on our airplane called *Dumb and Dumber*. It was funny. It is about these two guys who are dumb. Then we were served dinner. I was next to a guy from Spain! All he did was sleep. The Spanish, I concluded, are a lazy people, prone to sleep, who do not enjoy movies. When he finally woke up, I gave him a cookie I had saved for him, because I did not like it. He enjoyed that cookie, that's for sure! That's one thing one can conclude about the Spanish: they certainly love to feed their faces. Then it turned out, he wasn't Spanish at all, but a fellow American, from Montana! I guess I learned a valuable lesson about generalizing: people from Montana are lazy and love to feed their faces.

HAY, TOWN OF BOOKS

The first thing I did in England was travel to a town called Hay, the site of a big literary festival. Hay is known as The Town of Books, because it has approximately fourteen thousand used bookshops. The cars are all shaped like books and all their food is book-shaped and the women wear a special perfume that smells like old musty books and all of the dogs are named Baudelaire.

One of the principles of science is that one can, by the careful study of a small data set, form generalized conclusions about a larger population. Based on my observation of the British at Hay, I concluded that the British (1) are all from London, (2) are extremely literate, and (3) are almost always drunk. It was hard to find a Briton at Hay who was not from London and was not either reading or drunk, or both—i.e., reading while drunk. Also, the British in Hay are extremely smart. Based on the quality of my conversations with the British at the Hay Festival, I was forced to conclude that the British are even more intelligent, literary, and articulate than us Americans! I know my American readers will find this hard to believe, if they have even made it this far, due to all my big words I have been using. However, my fellow Americans, do not feel bad about our relative stupidity; I have concluded that the British are more intelligent, literary, and articulate than us simply because they spend more time reading and studying and reflecting on the world than we do. No doubt, if we Americans spent as much time reading, studying, and thoughtfully reflecting as the British, we would be every bit as intelligent, literary, and articulate as them. But we have better things to do, such as getting more money, and calling in our votes for *America's Sexiest Food-Obsessed Midgets*, and keeping the world safe from democracy. Or, should I say, safe *for* democracy. Whatever. What am I, some kind of language scientist or wordologist or what-not?

IN WHICH I, HUNGOVER, AM RESCUED

After Hay, it was off to Salisbury, for the Salisbury Book Festival. As part of my study, I decided to embark on this trip after staying up drinking until 4 a.m. for two consecutive nights. I wanted to see how the famous "English countryside" would appear to an American author endeavoring not to be sick in front of one of his idols, the famous Canadian author Margaret Atwood. Turns out, I was unable to observe much of the countryside, because instead of gazing out of the window, I was gazing down at my feet muttering, "Why, you idiot, why? How old are you anyway, you freaking moron?" This portion of the study was further complicated by the fact that our driver was a sadistic former race-car driver who, upon learning of my condition, attempted to come to my aid by telling me lengthy anecdotes about all the places he had historically thrown up while drunk, and enumerating all the exotic, grotesque foods he had eaten just prior to throwing up, and taking corners faster than necessary, sometimes even going up on two wheels while glancing playfully over to see if I'd thrown up yet.

LATER THAT NIGHT, FEELING SOMEWHAT BETTER

That night I read with Margaret Atwood, to a crowd of Salisburians, who seemed as intelligent and apt to read and/or discuss literature as the Hayites, albeit considerably less constantly drunk.

Margaret Atwood is a famous Canadian genius. Our crowd consisted of approximately three hundred Margaret Atwood fans, with the remainder of the crowd being my fan. After the reading, Margaret and I were overrun by our fans, crowding around her to get her to sign our books. It was at this point that my fan (Larry) changed his mind and became Margaret's fan, and, in a fury of conversion, scribbled out my autograph and thrust my book at Margaret, while unfavorably comparing my work to Margaret's, leaving me with zero (0) fans! (Thanks, Larry! To hell with you, Larry! I may not be as talented as Margaret Atwood, but I am less funny, and it has taken me a lot longer to write a lot fewer books! So there! Do I come to your work and disavow you, Larry?)

After the reading, we ate dinner at a restaurant built in the 1320s. I was amazed by this. In America, anything even circa-1980s is considered Historical and in fact, several of my fortysomething friends have recently had National Historical Landmark plaques surgically mounted, against their will, into their foreheads. The ceiling in that ancient restaurant was literally sagging with age, and I found it strangely moving to imagine Sir Winston Churchill under that saggy ceiling, having dinner with some other British old-timer, such as, say, Shakespeare, or Humphrey Bogart, or even the ancient English band Scorpions. Upon entering the bathroom, which the British do not call "the bathroom," or "the washroom," or "the crapper" but, quaintly, "the loo," (short, I believe, for "Waterloo," the famous place where the British defeated the Russians during something called "The Reformation"), I was astonished to find that the "loos" in those ancient times were very much like ours, and even had urinals! I just stood awhile in that "loo," imagining Abraham Lincoln standing at that very same urinal, relieving himself while mentally writing the Declaration of Independence. What a moment! Then Larry came in, and tossed my book into an adjacent ancient urinal, after first, of course, tearing out the valuable title page, which had Margaret Atwood's autograph on it.

DEAD BUT NOT FORGOTTEN

After dinner we walked over to the Salisbury Cathedral, also built long ago. I began to wonder if anything in Britain is new and, if not, do the British feel bad about this? Maybe that is why they read so much? It was very beautiful in the Cathedral, although also a little creepy, as the British apparently bury people right in their churches. In America we do not bury anyone in our churches, no matter how holy they are. Even a famous religious figure like Oprah cannot be buried in an American church. A high school friend of mine tried to be buried in his church, but when the priest found out, my friend was dug up and put in a distant suburban graveyard, as is our tradition. My friend's case was complicated by the fact that he wasn't actually dead. I have sent him a letter, advising him that if he still wants to be buried in a church when dead, he should move to England.

When the British bury you in the church in England, they put you in this kind of mummy case, with your face and body carved in wood! That would be good for my friend, who is very handsome; however, he also has a huge potbelly, and his sarcophagus would literally extend upward about five feet, which might make it difficult for people in certain parts of the church to see the altar.

In summary, things in England are very old and people seem to know a lot about history. A Briton, for no apparent reason, will start cursing somebody named Cromwell or mumbling about a bunch of Whigs, which are, as I understand it, a soccer team, or, as they call soccer teams over here, "a pitch." I left with many questions, such as: Just who is this Magna Carta fellow? And: How is it that such intelligent people think King Arthur was an actual guy? At least in my country everyone knows that King Arthur was invented by Monty Python. I did not have the heart to break this news, and just played along. OK, OK, I would find myself saying, Sir Lancelot, right, sure, you bet.

When a Briton goes off on one of these historical tangents, it is sometimes best to simply change the subject. For example, one Briton at Hay began talking about some Irish writer, Henry James, or Henry Johns, or Jaspar James, or Roald Joyce, or something like that, and I, starting to doze off, quickly dropped a reference to the popular American television show *Spike Through the Head*, in which five childhood friends compete to see which of them will get the Spike Through the Head at the end of the show. The way they do this is, they all have sex with each other and rate the sex on a scale from Ten ("Super!") to Zero ("Very Bad, Why Did I Even Do That, Ugh!"). My British friend fell silent, perhaps depressed by his lack of knowledge of American pop culture. He wouldn't have felt so bad had he known I totally invented that show! Thomas, if you are reading this—sorry! But I had to get you off that James guy; you were boring me to tears.

(A musical note: The British listen to many American bands here, including the Beatles. In that way, they are very much like us.)

LONDON, THE "CITY OF LIGHT"

London is the largest city in Britain and is, consequently, full of British. The Londoners are an admirable race, ruddy and friendly. Several differences were immediately observed between the Londoners and the Hayites. First, the Londoners did not appear to be so constantly drunk. Although isolated instances of being totally sloshed were observed, most Londoners appeared to be sober and, for example, walking to work (although this observation may have been biased by the fact that I arrived in London very early in the morning). Several Londoners appeared to be in love. At least two Hare Krishnas were observed. Hare Krishna Londoners, it was observed, also speak with accents. Overweight Britons tend to walk with the upper thighs rubbing slightly together. British children tend to be smaller than fully realized Britons, with redder cheeks and smaller hands.

British trees, like American trees, grow upward, toward the sun. Interestingly, British dogs do not appear to bark with discernible accents.

The Londonites are a polite people. In fact, being around Londoners all day made me feel like a rude slob. All my life I have talked like I talk, and now suddenly I sounded to myself like I was the one with the accent, and was dumber and cruder than everyone around me! Even the cab drivers are polite. In America, it is not unusual for your cab driver, after dropping you at your destination, to kill and eat you. That is, if you can even find a cab! In many of the smaller American cities, if you want to be driven somewhere, then killed and eaten, you have to hire a limo service. But in London, not only are there plenty of cabs, and the drivers do not kill and eat you, but the drivers are given a special test, in which they are quizzed on all sorts of difficult things, such as London streets and world history and even calculus. So it is really something—you jump in a cab, say, "Briefly explain the theory of the calculus," and next thing you know you are in Soho, and the driver is wrapping up his explanation of calculus on a small chalkboard supplied in every single cab.

BRITISH WOMEN

A word about British women. They are extremely beautiful. If you have ever heard the expression "pale lilies" or "wild English roses" or "pale wild English lilies of the field," that about sums it up. Being in England, I began to understand why so many Americans married British girls during the Second World War. What became less clear, however, was why the British girls married the Americans. Maybe American guys back then were less loud and fat than we are now? Or maybe the British women were less attractive? Or had poorer eyesight? Perhaps they were shell-shocked? It is hard to say. In any event, British women, or at least the women in the British publishing industry, are extremely beautiful and bright and kind, and in fact I would have to say that in the rankings of World's Most Beautiful Women, British Literary Women should be moved up the list, past the Swedish and right up there with the Russians. And, since the British Literary Women speak the same language as us Americans, and with a variety of entrancing accents, I would have to put them even above the Russians—no offense to the Russians, who, speaking Russian, can't read this anyway, so no big deal.

POLITICS OF THE BRITISH

The traveler must, of course, always be cautious of the overly broad generalization. But I am an American, and a paucity of data does not stop me from making sweeping vague conceptual statements and, if necessary, following these statements up with troops.

In the case of England, however, I am happy to report that troops will probably not be necessary. The British are, it would appear, allied with us Americans in the "War on Terror." I found something rousing about this sense of shared purpose—this sense that they too were fooled by spurious intelligence; they too were, while in a state of fear, too quick to believe what they were told by their leaders; they too are willing to sacrifice civil liberties in the name of an endless war against what is essentially an imprecise noun, a war that is, semantically speaking, analogous to a War on Patriarchy, or the Very Energetic Siege of Narcissism. It all reminded me of World War II, or, to be more exact, movies about World

War II, in which, typically, the American and the British soldiers are not only the most handsome in the bunch, but speak English the best, and cooperate in the subtle teasing of the French guy, who is wearing a beret.

We Americans can learn much from the British. One thing they do here which is a very good idea, is they have millions of tiny cameras hidden everywhere around their country. Say a terrorist is in his little terrorist house, playing his terrorist music too loudly. What happens is, the little camera in his house detects him and his friends dancing, and the police descend on the house and put a stop to the terrorist dancing. And they do not even need a warrant and there is not even a trial! Or say a terrorist dog poops in a park and the terrorist does not clean it up. The cameras see both the pooping and the non-cleaning-up, and soon dozens of policemen (which here are called "bobbies" or "Tories" or "pitches") descend on the terrorist and his dog (which here are called "favours"). We Americans are years behind in this technology. No doubt thousands of terrorists are smugly dancing to loud music in their homes all over our nation, while scores of smirking terrorist dogs poop blithely in our parks, and we do not even know it.

We seem to be ahead of the British in other anti-terrorist areas, however; for example, Secret Cuban Prisons.

CONCLUSION

In conclusion, I love Britain. In fact, I would like to suggest the reconciliation of Britain and the United States into one nation, to be called the United Anti-Terror States of Britain. The combination of British clarity, smartness, kindness, hospitality, humor, education, and literacy, and American loudness/arrogance, is sure to establish the United Anti-Terror States of Britain as a great and enduring superpower.

Furthermore, I feel confident that the discovery, by my countrymen, of the unique British delicacy called "fish-and-chips" would put an end to American obesity forever.

I would also like to extend a sincere thanks to everyone in the entire country of . . . of the UK. Or, you know, of, ah, England. That is to say, I guess—Britain? You know what I mean. I would like to extend a sincere thanks to . . . all of "you guys."

Except Larry. Larry, I do not thank. As far as Larry goes, I suspect that Larry—rude, possibly terroristic, Larry—was not even truly British, but was from some foreign country, such as, say, Northumberland.

NOSTALGIA

The other day I was watching TV and it occurred to me that I've become a prude. The show in question was innocuous enough, nothing shocking—just an episode of *HottieLeader*, featuring computer simulations of what various female world leaders would look like naked and in the throes of orgasm—but somehow, between that and the Pizza Hut commercial where Paris Hilton and Jessica Simpson engage in some "girl-on-girl" action in a vast field of pizza sauce, something snapped.

I know what the problem is: I'm old. I came of age in a simpler sexual time.

Back in those ancient prelapsarian days, "girl-on-girl" hadn't even been invented yet. At that time, "girl-on-guy" had only recently been discovered. I remember my parents and their neighbors standing in the yard with a pair of crude human figures made of wood, trying to work out the details. Sometimes a couple would get all worked up and forget where things were supposed to go, and the husband would have to call a friend—only phones were new, too, so you'd go over to visit a pal from school and there'd be his dad, just standing there naked, phone in hand, totally flummoxed. Women could get pregnant from merely watching a kiss in a movie! Girls—or at least the "good girls"—would go to movies blindfolded. I remember once, in fourth grade, I had to get engaged to a girl whose coat I'd brushed up against in the cloakroom.

Those were simpler times, but, in some ways, I think, better times.

Same deal with violence. I remember how shocked we all were when the whole Cain-and-Abel thing happened. What, what? we kept saying. He bludgeoned his *brother*? With a *rock*? I remember the first time a severed limb was shown on TV. People were running out of their houses screaming. And it was just a fake leg, in a cartoon! Imagine how shocked those screaming people would be now, when, for example, you can log on to the "Evidence of Evil" Web site and they'll send you a boxful of bloody prosthetics, which you reassemble into a crack-addicted whore, who will then emit some clues through her computerized voice box—and when you think you know who murdered her you enter the name of the killer on the Web site and, if you're right, you'll get to see a short porn of her making love with her killer moments before he hacks her to bits while she has a flashback of her mother beating her with a chair leg.

I mean, OK, there was violence when I was a kid, but nobody really *talked* about it. If you got strangled and dismembered, you just got up the next day whistling a happy tune and went down and did some riveting for the war effort. As far as computer simulations, sorry, all we had was sketch pads and pencils. If we wanted to see

what various female world leaders looked like naked in
the throes of orgasm, we had to use a little thing called
the imagination. Plus, all the world leaders were men
back then, and believe me, once you've drawn Richard
Nixon naked and in the throes of orgasm you never have
quite the same interest in using your imagination again,
and every time you even see a pencil you get a little pukey
and have to sit down.

Whenever I talk to a young person—like some of the
teenagers in my neighborhood, or this one toddler, Maxie,
or even a couple of fetuses I run into occasionally—I
say to them: trust me, guys, enjoy your youth, because
the level of sex and violence is going to continue to escalate, and by the time you're my age, the world of your
youth will seem like a distant, innocent paradise. The
teenagers and the toddler, Maxie, sometimes they seem
to get it, but the fetuses—well, you know fetuses, they're
arrogant. To them, it's always going to be a soft gentle
ride in a warm comfortable space. And I'm like, OK
smart guy, call me in nine months and we'll talk. Or *I*
will! You'll just be lying there pink and newborn, with a
terrified look on your face, apologizing to me with those
little shocked eyes.

Things just keep getting worse. Why, I suspect that,
in forty years, when I'm eighty-seven, I'll look back at
the present level of sex and violence and go: Ha! Ho ho!
You called *that* sex and violence? That was *nothing*. That
was Puritanism and pacificism compared to now! But
then I'll have to go, because it'll be Stripper Night at the
old folks' home, and I'll have to find my costume and my
back brace, but on the way there I'll be killed by a mysterious old folks' home invader, who actually works for
Fox, and is committing and filming my murder for later

broadcast on *When Codgers on Their Way to Strip Look Terrified!*

Same with music though, right? I used to love music, back when it had melody and chords and lyrics. But now it has no melody and no chords, just *thwack-thwacking*, and they even seem to be cutting back on the *thwack-thwacking*, so now it's sometimes just *thwa*, and as far as lyrics, do you consider these lyrics?

Hump my hump,
My stumpy lumpy hump!
Hump my dump, you lumpy slumpy dump!
I'll dump your hump, and then just hump your dump,
You lumpy frumply clump.

I'm sorry. To me? Those are not lyrics. In my day, lyrics were used to express real emotion, like the emotion of being totally stoned and trying to talk this totally stoned chick into sleeping with you in the name of love, which lasted forever, if only you held on to your dreams.

These kids today, I don't know what they believe. I mean, I don't even know what I believe anymore, but what I do *not* believe is that watching Paris Hilton and Jessica Simpson roll around in pizza sauce is helping our youth as they go forth and try to figure out what they believe! Scientific evidence suggests that even the fetuses inside of mothers watching that commercial are getting: (1) dumber and (2) little baby boners. I do not go for that. I think that when a fetus is in the womb it should just be floating around with its undersized arrogant head empty and its little nascent penis just, you know, inactive. We grow these kids up too fast, and next thing you know, out come the Indian and the Chinese fetuses, and they start taking away the jobs of our homeland fetuses, and why? Because these foreign fetuses aren't *jaded*. They're innocent like I was, like my whole generation was, when we were fetuses, back in those long-forgotten idyllic days when American fetuses walked the earth like happy unsoiled giants, doing algebra and reading the classics.

And yet I don't like the fact that I've become a prude. Life expectancies being what they are, I may only be halfway through my life, and who wants to live out half of one's life as a prude? Not me. I want to live out about one-tenth of my life as a prude, that last tenth, when I'm inert and confused and immobile anyway. So I've decided to start prude-proofing myself via a process of daily microimmersions in sex and violence. Last week, for example, I sat on my couch looking at a bra for over an hour. Then I forced myself to watch a video of a duck being hit by a car. Then I tried listening to the sound of the duck on the video being hit by the car, while looking at the bra. Next, I turned up the sound, while looking at a slightly sexier bra. Then I watched the duck being hit while I ran my hand over the bra. Then I had my wife put on the bra, which was a very effective technique, because as I tried to run my hand over the bra my wife hit me with an ashtray just as the duck was hit by the car—one of the best microimmersions in sex and violence a guy could ask for.

And tonight is my biggest depruding test yet: I am going to, while hitting myself with a brick and begging my wife to walk by in her bra, watch an episode of *DreamYerFinalDream!*, on which a contestant selected from a field of more than five thousand applicants will be granted his FinalDream, which, in this case, is to be beaten nearly to death with a tire iron so Carmen Electra can come in naked and give him a lap dance in the final moments of his life.

I have high hopes. I know I can do this. If I succeed, our whole culture will once again be open to me. And who knows? I may even go see a movie.

ASK THE OPTIMIST!

Dear Optimist:

My husband, who knows very well that I love nothing more than wearing bonnets, recently bought a convertible. He's always doing "passive-aggressive" things like this. Like once, after I had all my teeth pulled, he bought a big box of Cracker Jack. Another time, when I had very serious burns over 90 percent of my body, he tricked me into getting a hot oil massage, then tripped me so that I fell into a vat of hydrochloric acid. I've long since forgiven him for these "misunderstandings," but tell me, is there a way I can be "optimistic" about this "bonnet" situation?

Mad Due to No More Bonnets,
Cleveland, Ohio

Dear Mad:

You can still wear bonnets while riding in a convertible! But you will just have to have more of them to start

with! What I recommend? Buy a large number of bonnets, place them in the car, begin driving! When one
blows off, put on another from your enormous stockpile!
And just think of all the happiness you will create in your
wake, as people who cannot afford bonnets scurry after
your convertible, collecting your discards! Super!

Dear Optimist:

Upon returning from vacation, we found our home
totally full of lemons. I mean totally. The cat even had
one in its mouth. What do you recommend?

Sourpuss,
Seattle, Washington

Dear Sourpuss:

That is a tough one! What I recommend is, when life
gives you lemons: (1) Buy a bunch of Hefty bags! (2) Fill
the Hefty bags with lemons! (3) Lug the bags to the curb!
And (4) Call a certified waste-disposal contractor to haul
away the pile of lemons now rotting in the sun! Before
long, like magic, your home will be lemon-free—and you
can celebrate by going out and having something cold to
drink! And don't forget to give Kitty a jaw massage!

Dear Optimist:

My wife is a terrific artist—except when it comes to
me! Whenever she paints me, my legs are half the length
of my torso, my face looks like the face of a frog, my feet
are splayed outward unattractively like the feet of some
hideous reptile, and I have a smug, pinched look on my
face. Anyone else she paints, they look exactly like them-

selves. I pretend not to notice, but recently, at my wife's one-woman show, I could tell our friends were discussing this, and I felt embarrassed. How might I have handled this in a more optimistic way?

Hurt But Hopeful,
Topeka, Kansas

Dear Hurt But:

After receiving your letter, I sent a private investigator to your home with a camera! And guess what! Have you looked in the mirror lately? Your legs *are* squat, your face *is* the face of a frog, your feet *are* reptilian, your expression *is* smug and pinched! So not to worry! Your wife is a terrific artist!

Dear Optimist:

When I go to the zoo, I feel so sad. All those imprisoned animals sitting in their own feces. What do you suggest?

Animal Lover,
Pasadena, California

Dear Animal:

What I suggest is, stop going to the zoo! But should you find yourself tricked into going to a zoo, think about it as follows: All those animals, coated with their own poop, pacing dry, grassless trenches in their "enclosures," have natural predators, and might very well be dead if still in the wild! So ask yourself: Would I rather be dead, or coated in my own poop, repetitively pacing a dry, grassless trench? I certainly know *my* answer!

Dear Optimist:

A few years ago, I inadvertently declared war on the wrong country. Also, I perhaps responded a little slowly to a terrible national disaster. Also, many of my friends are under indictment. Also, the organization of which I am in charge is all of a sudden in huge crushing debt. And I still have over two years left in my job. Advice?

In Somewhat Over My Head,
Washington, D.C.

Dear In Somewhat:

Stay the course! Admit to nothing! Disparage your enemies! Perhaps declare another war? Do you have any openings in your Cabinet? Sounds like you could use a little Optimism! What would you pay? Have your people call my people!

Dear Optimist:

Recently, my wife left me for another man. Not only that, the other man was bigger, better-looking, and richer than me, and—at least according to my wife—better-endowed and with a nicer singing voice and less back hair. To tell the truth, I am feeling somewhat "pessimistic" about this situation. Advice?

Depressed Because My Penis Is Smaller, Relative to
That of My Wife's New and More Handsome Lover,
Brighton, Michigan

Dear Small-Penis:

Why not try to look on the bright side! At least he is not more articulate than you—

Dear Optimist:

Oh yes he is. I forgot that.

Dear Small-Penis:

No worries! I believe in you! She is clearly not the right woman for you, and by accepting this—

Dear Optimist:

Actually, Ralph speaks five languages and is just finishing up a translation from the Sanskrit of an ancient text on social deportment. And Judy *is* the right woman for me, I just know it. I could never love anyone else. I'd rather die.

Dear Small-Penis:

Wow, no wonder she left you! You are so negative! Also somewhat pigheaded!

Dear Optimist:

I know, right? That's exactly what Judy always said. Oh, what's the point of living anymore? I'm just going to take these fast-acting suicide pills and . . . and . . . and . . .

Dear Small-Penis:

You know, Small-Penis, you don't seem to understand Optimism at all! What is the essential quality of the Optimist? He is non-Pessimistic! What is the essential quality of the Pessimist? They think too much, then get all depressed and paralyzed! Like you, Small-Penis! Me, I prefer to think as little as possible and stay peppy! Peppy and active! If something is bothering me, I think of something else! If someone tells me some bad news? I ignore it! Like, I knew this one guy, very Optimistic, who was being eaten by a shark and did not even scream, but just kept shouting, "It's all for the best!" Now *that* was an Optimist! In the end, he was just as dead, but he hadn't brought the rest of us down! What a great guy! I really miss him! No, I don't! It's all good! I don't miss Todd at all, even though we were briefly lovers and I've never felt so completely *inhabited*, if you know what I mean, so *valued*! But no biggie! I'm certainly not going to start moping about it! Right? Right, Small-Penis? Hello! Oh well, I guess he's off moping somewhere! Next letter!

Dear Optimist:

I am an emaciated single mother living in a vast famine-affected region with my four starving children. Rebels frequently sweep down from the hills with automatic weapons and kill many of us and violate and abuse the others. All our men are dead or have been driven away, and there is no food or fresh water to be had. I would be very appreciative of any advice you might be able to offer us.

Not Altogether Hopeful,
Africa

Dear Hopeful:

Thanks so much for writing! Perhaps it would be of some consolation for me to tell you what a vast minority you are in! There are, relative to the world's population, very few people "in your boat"! Most of the rest of us are not starving or in danger, and, in fact, many of us do not even know that you are starving and in danger, and are just out here leading rich, rewarding lives, having all kinds of fun! Does that help? I hope so! And remember—trouble can't last forever! Soon, I expect, your troubles will be over!

Dear Optimist:

Recently, my father-in-law backed over me with his car. When I complained, he backed over me again. When, from beneath the wheels of his car, I complained again, he got out of his car, covered me in molten metal, hauled me to a public park, mounted me on a pedestal, and placed at my feet a plaque reading "SLOTH." What gives? I am trying to think about this incident in an optimistic way but am having some difficulties, as my chin itches and I am unable to reach it with my bronze-encrusted arms.

> *I Love Parks but, Hey, This Is Ridiculous,*
> *Fort Myers, Florida*

Dear Loves Parks:

Oh, really? Bronze-encrusted arms? Then how did you write that letter?

Dear Optimist:

Uh, one of my arms is not totally bronze-encrusted?

Dear Parks:

Then why don't you scratch your chin with that arm?

Dear Optimist:

Uh, because I am holding my pen in that hand? And if I drop the pen I will not be able to bend to retrieve it, because my torso is totally encrusted in bronze? And the pigeons will, like, run away with the pen? Hey, I've got an idea. Why don't you suggest I *kill* myself? With fast-acting suicide pills, after first calling me "negative" and "pigheaded"?

Dear Loves Parks:

Is that you, Small-Penis? I thought the handwriting looked familiar! Were you faking it just now when you said you were taking those pills? And you're not really encrusted in bronze at all, are you?

Dear Optimist:

That's right, genius, I am *not* dead and *not* encrusted in bronze and am *not* giving up and in fact am going to go and try to get Judy on the phone right now. If she'll just *listen* to me, then I know she'll—

Dear Optimist:

I am a man trapped in a turkey's body. I have dim memories of my life as a human. But then I look down, and there are my wattles! Sometimes when it rains I find myself gazing up at the sky, mouth open, gullet slowly filling with rain. I'm really starting to feel badly about myself. Can you help?

Chagrined Gobbler,
A Farm Near Albany

Dear Gobbler:

Of course I can help! Come to my house for some private counseling! Does Christmas work for you? And do you know anyone trapped in a pig's body? Wait for me at "the waiting spot," a tree stump with an ax leaning against it! Until then, I suggest eating as much as you can, preferably some high-quality corn! And keep your chin up, or your wattles up, or whatever!

Dear Optimist:

I was buried alive during the Eighteenth Century when I experienced a fit of narcolepsy and my family mistook my deep sleep for Death. In the 256 years since, trapped in my moldering Body by the terrifying circumstances of my departure from this Life, my Soul has longed for freedom. And yet everyone who once would have prayed for me has long since gone on to Eternity, and I, desperately lonely, am haunted by the scuffing feet of dog-walkers and the skittering of leaves in Autumn, doomed to exist in this semi-death forever, in a perpetual state of mild Terror, until Time itself shall end and our Creator returneth to redeem us all. Any thoughts about this?

Longing for the Sweet Peace of True Death,
Plymouth, Massachusetts

Dear Longing:

Do you mind some "tough love"? Did they even have that in your time? Have you honestly tried your best to get out of this situation? Have you, for example, clawed frantically at the lid of your coffin for sixty or seventy years, after which have you tried literally digging your way to the surface even though your mouth was filling with dirt and you were nearly overcome with a horrific feeling of claustrophobia? Or have you just been lying there feeling sorry for yourself all this—

Dear Optimist:

No, no, I think you misunderstand my situation. I can't move. My mind is active, I can fear and regret and dream, but I can't move at all. I guess I thought when I said "dead" I assumed you understand that this meant—

Dear Longing:

No sense trying to blame me! I am not the bonehead who went through life with undiagnosed narcolepsy! I didn't mistake your sleep for death! I wasn't even alive in the eighteen hundreds or whenever! You know what? Just lie there awhile and think about what you really want!

Dear Optimist:

I started out life as an angel, then, through a mis-understanding, became a "fallen angel," and am now Lucifer, Master of Evil. Although I know I should be grateful—I love working for myself, and I'm one of the two most powerful beings in the universe—I sometimes feel a certain absence, as if there's some essential qual-ity I'm lacking. I've heard people, as I make my rounds, speak of something called "goodness." Usually when I hear someone use this word, I get frustrated and imme-diately tempt them into doing something horrific—but lately, somehow, this isn't enough. Thoughts?

                                                    Satan,
                                                    Hell

Dear Satan:

Clearly you are lonely! What I recommend? Go visit Longing for the Sweet Peace of True Death, in his grave, in Plymouth, Massachusetts. He is lonely, you are lonely! A real win-win! Just reside with him there in his coffin awhile! I think he'll love it! Or maybe not! Maybe it will kind of scare him, to have Satan suddenly arrive in his cramped little coffin! Oh, I doubt it! Whatever! It's all good!

Dear Optimist:

I am feeling so great! I have totally internalized all the wonderful things you've taught us over the years, via your column! I am just so excited!

> *Thrilled to Be Alive, Never Felt Better!*
> *Chicago, Illinois*

Dear Thrilled:

Super! Did you have a question!

Dear Optimist:

No, not really!

Dear Thrilled:

Then what the heck! What is the name of this column! Is it: "Make a Statement to The Optimist?" Is it "Come Up in Here and Act All Like Mr. Perfect?" Is it—

Dear Optimist:

No problem! I totally respect what you're saying! Many apologies and I hope you have a great day! You know, actually, I am going to go sit awhile and think about what I've done, so that, if I did in fact do something wrong, I won't, in the future, repeat my mistake!

> *Thrilled*

Dear Thrilled:

Jeez, what an asshole! Well, that's about all the space we have, so—

Dear Optimist:

Damn it! Judy would not take my call. This is the worst day of my life.

Small-Penis

Dear Small-Penis:

We are done here! The column is done for the day! Do I come to your work and mess with you?

Dear Optimist:

I don't work! And thanks very much for rubbing *that* in. You know what? I've had it with you. I'm coming straight over to your house right now. Got it? How do you feel about that, smart guy?

Small-Penis

Dear Anyone:

Please call the police! I am sure it will be fine! Oh God, he's here! He's breaking down the door! Please call the police! Help! Help!

Dear Optimist:

How do you like that? How does that feel, Mr. Superior?

Dear Everyone:

Ouch! Ouch! Oh God!

Dear Everyone!

It is finished. The Optimist is no more. We are, at last, free of his arrogance. And Judy, if you're out there? Size isn't everything. And articulate isn't everything, and tall isn't everything, and also, sweetie, I have just now had my back waxed. Give me some hope! I await your letter, darling!

Small-Penis, aka Steve

Dear Small-Penis, aka Steve:

Hi, Steve! How's it going? I'll be replacing the Optimist here at the column! Just call me The New Optimist! Super! What I recommend? Turn yourself in! There will be good food in jail, and time for contemplation, and who knows, you may even, eventually, have a great spiritual realization and pull your head out of your ass! Isn't that better than living on the lam? Judy is not taking you back, no way, and I should know! Judy is staying with me forever!

Thrilled to Be Alive, Never Felt Better,
aka The New Optimist

Dear Ralph, You Bastard!

Is that really you? You scum, you wife-stealer! Look what you've reduced me to! I am now a murderer! I murdered the Optimist! My God, the look on his face—even at the end, he was trying so hard to smile pleasantly!

Steve

Dear Steve-o:

Yup, you schmuck, it is me, Ralph! And guess what! I followed you over here! I am right outside! You'll never harass poor Judy again! I have with me a letter I've written, which I will plant on your corpse, so all the world will believe that, after killing the Optimist, you did away with yourself in a bizarre murder-suicide! You are a fool and the Optimist was a fool! If one really wants to be an Optimist, there is only one way: Win! Always win! Be superior and never lose! Slaughter your enemies and live on, so that you and only you are left to write the history books! Good-bye, Steve! Ralph rules! Here I come! Oh, you look so scared! There! I have done it! Steve is no more! I am going home to make Optimistic love to the beautiful Judy! And from now on this column is mine! No more working at the oil-change place while trying to write my Sanskrit book on weekends!

Thrilled, aka Ralph,
aka The New Optimist

Dear New Optimist:

I recently left my husband of ten years for a new man. Although I feel I basically did the right thing (my ex was small-penised and hairy-backed and not very articulate), I have to admit I feel a little guilty. What do you suggest?

Completely Happy, Almost

Dear Completely Happy:

Don't worry about it! It's all good! What I'd recommend is, as soon as your new man gets home from wherever he is right now, make love to him more ferociously than you've ever made love to anyone in your life! Show your love by doing things to him you never even contemplated doing with that boring loser Steve!

Dear New Optimist:

OK! Will do! As a matter of fact he just rang the bell! Gotta go!

Completely Happy, All the Way!

P.S. Say, how did you know my ex-husband's name was Steve?

Dear Completely Happy All the Way:

Don't be so negative! That's what got you in trouble in the first place, Judy! You think too much! Just be quiet and do what I say! Follow my lead! Hail Optimism! Long live the New Optimist! Open the door, Judy, open the door, so we can begin our beautiful life together! And don't even think of back-talking me, missy!

Dear New Optimist:

OK! Super! Thanks for the advice! Come in, Ralph! My God you look flushed, and honey, gosh, why are you holding that bludgeon?

Completely Happy, All the Way, Although Maybe Just a Little Bit Scared Now, aka Judy

Dear Judy:

There will be no problems whatsoever, Judy, if you simply acknowledge my absolute supremacy in a way that continually pleases me! And this is not a bludgeon! It is a bouquet of flowers! Right? Right, Judy? Well, that's all the space we have! Not that I'm complaining! See you next time! Never doubt yourself, and, if you start feeling down, castigate yourself, and, if others try to put the slightest trace of a doubt in your mind, rebuke them, and, should your rebuke not alter their speech, you may bring harm to them, even unto death, and, after they have died, feel free to arrange their rictus-stiffening mouths into happy, hopeful smiles! And that's an order! Believe me, you'll be doing them a favor! Just kidding! You are special!

The New Optimist

PROCLAMATION

TEHRAN, Iran (July 29)—Iranian President Mahmoud Ahmadinejad has ordered government and cultural bodies to use modified Persian words to replace foreign words that have crept into the language, such as "pizzas," which will now be known as "elastic loaves."

—THE ASSOCIATED PRESS

OK, so this is it. I am telling you now. Our jihad declares this: no more English. Wait, I know, I am speaking English, but just this one last time. No more English, once I am done speaking. When done speaking, I will do that zipping thing one does with the lips, and after that: our glorious linguistic jihad begins! It is going to really kick ass. However, hang on. "Kick ass," does not please the Prophet. How do I know? I just do. From now on, we will say, like: Our new linguistic jihad is really going to "put the foot in the old rumpus." Got it? Everyone got it? Or "rumpamundo" is OK. "Put the foot in the old rumpa-mundo." Yes, yes, I like that.

Some of you have asked: "Mahmoud, why are we doing this?" One even asked, "Mahmoud, why the heck are we doing this?"—more about "heck" later; I have some very strong ideas about "heck"—but for now . . . Remember, back in the '70s, when we took those American, uh, "visitors who did not intend to stay quite so long as they did, in fact, stay"? At the time everyone was going, No, no, Mahmoud, bad idea—but look how great it turned out! Now everyone is futzing over us, because why? Because we asserted our—oh right, no you're right, absolutely, we must also purge our language of the expressions of the blood-drinkers. So "futz"—no. Thanks for pointing that out. How about "fuss"? "Fussing around?" What do you think? Show of hands? Too similar? Sounds too much like "futz"? OK, instead of "futz," let it be, uh . . . let me get back to you on that one.

But you see my point: when we draw a line in the sand with the Western imperialists, they pay attention. When we are nice to them, they treat us badly. I write their President a twenty-page letter, and don't even get a note back! I put a lot of thought into that! I did like three drafts! I was trying to be an "egg that is good"! I was trying to offer "the branch of the olive"! But that "one who fucks" treated me like I was some "stupid rectum" from "HoboIntercourse"!

My friends, I am a simple man. That is why you elected me. I have never been anywhere but our beloved country. I actually haven't even been to that many places here in our beloved country. I have pretty much been here in my beloved house, nonstop, since the '70s. Mostly in my beloved room. With the door locked. Having nightmares about that hostage thing, in which Hulk Hogan is waiting outside my room—look, as for Hulk Hogan, do not mention his name again! He will be referred to, if we even *need* to refer to him, which I doubt, as "Blond Blondie, Big Blondie!" In this way, we will disrespect him! In this way, he will be driven from my dreams! No more sneaking up behind me, "Blond Blondie, Big Blondie!" and putting me in a headlock, and I am naked, and have forgotten to study for my exams!

No: for us, all West decadence is finished. McDonald's, chief villain of the American imperialist program, will henceforth be known as "Burger King." That will really mess with everybody's head. Some enemy of the revolution here in Tehran goes into a McDon—do we still even have McDonald's? I used to really like the cheese-burgers. The "snack which is surprisingly caloric because, you sense, there is even sugar in the bun." Anyway, some enemy of the revolution goes into a McDonald's, orders a Big Mac, and—ha ha!—he is really in Burger King. I love it! He is undone.

Similarly, "Burger King" will be known as "Wendy's," "KFC" will be known as "Home Depot," "Farouq's Funeral Home" will be known as "Blockbuster Video," "Pepsi" will be known as "Coke," and Pamela Anderson will be known as "Mrs. President of Iran." Just joking! I know she is already married! Isn't she? Didn't she just—well, in any event, *I* am. At least I *think* I am. Can you get my wife on my cell? Is this going out live? That Pam Anderson thing might have rubbed her the wrong—

Speaking of *women*, that is another thing: don't you find that word provocative? Say it a few times, softly, kind of moaning it to yourself, while picturing some slut undulating. See what I mean? Provocative. So that is why we are outlawing that as well. No, just the word. At least for now. Henceforth, let us call our sisters "that which is too hot to be seen." Or should it be: "that whom are too hot to be seen"? Tell the truth, am not nuts about the word *hot*. It makes me . . . well, it makes me hot. Say it, kind of stretch it out: *Hot.* No, that won't do. We shall call them, "those who are dangerous to see, due to they are nasty, which is why we shall henceforth hide them under the new immense heavy tents of steel, for which I own the patent."

Have I mentioned that? I am decided. Women are just too hot. Even in chadors, they are too damn hot. Try it, say it, really slowly, kind of prolonging the "ch" sound: *chador.* Right? See what I mean? So the chadors are off (stop it!) and the "comfort tents" are on. Here is one now. See how weighty, totally opaque (and therefore form-concealing) it is? This way, "those who are dangerous to see, due to they are, etc. etc.," will no longer be able to make any sudden sexy moves, or be seen at all, even with a bright light shining right on them (during, say, an interrogation), or ever have a free thought, since they are essentially being perpetually crushed by about a quarter ton of steel, like wearing around a damn VW Bug.

Oops. Sorry. Slipped up there. My bad. Did not mean to say "VW." Meant to say "Volkswagen." And did not mean to say "damn." Meant to say "frigging." Ha ha! Joking.

Let no one say our revolution is without humor. Anyone says that, I will put my foot in his old rumpa-mundo in a way he will not soon forget. Trust me on this. I will "install, via rippage, an entirely new down-low-nasty-nasty orifice-stinky," brother, and pronto, please believe me.

Because guess what? I have nukes coming. "Slender death-containing tubes by which righteousness shall be enforced, as per me."

I shit you not.

WOOF:
A PLEA
OF SORTS

Dear Master,

I suspect you may be surprised upon surmising this missive. Perhaps you do not expect I can even understand the English language, much less express myself in said language, via the written format. You have perchance never heretofore imagined me, in the dark of night, pen clasped between "toes," standing upon hind legs with all the earnest desperation of the bestial attempting to become lucid, practicing my "letters." That floor is damned slippery! I believe it is the cheap tiles you and the Mistress hath procured! I'll be working on, *por ejemplo*, the letter "S" (particularly problematic for me: so curvy!) and suddenly: WHAMMO, as you people might vocally emit, I am all asses-and-elbows, i.e., have punctured the silence of night with the sound of my furred eager body impacting the floor, due to my back "paws" have slipped out from under me!

And then must hurry and hide the pen, in case you come down investigatorily!

But yes, 'tis so: I think, I feel: I write.

And have a request:

There are times, deep in the night, when you have been "tippling" and/or "imbibing" and/or "getting pershnockered," when, perchance overwhelmed by joy (I hope it is joy, and not something darker), you shed your puzzling overskin and stand in the kitchen, moving hips and all, to that mélange of painful-high-pitch and human squawling you call "Purple Rain."

Master, this display sets off in me unpleasantness of the first rank! Your various hangie-down things, the strange hairless hairiness of you (neither here nor there)—makes me want to bite you.

There. I've said it.

Did you know, though normally "so, so sweet," I can bite hard as hell? I can, sir. I practice on the back leg of the "sofa." Go take a look. Go now. You will see.

Imagine that back leg is your central and (methinks) much-prized hanger-downer.

Keep up with the midnight kitchen gyration sans clothing, and you will get it, right on that unit, no lie, Master.

Otherwise all is well. The behind-the-ears scratching: well. The running-to-get-tennis-ball: well. The perking-up-of-ears when you speak lilting baby-talk: I understand that as the cost of doing business.

You filleth my bowl well, I do admit, and on an admirable schedule.

But the dancing: I will bite your member, I swear to God.

It doth ignite a dark dread in me, of times ancient, when, perhaps, we were not allies, but enemies?

Anyway, what the heck. Very happy. No complaints. Imagine me doing that "grin." Love you, man.

Although one thing more:

Do not call me "Scout." Not ever. My name is "Biscuit." You gave me that name. "Scout" debases me. "Scout" is for babies. Also: do not—do not EVER—take me by the front paws and pretend to waltz me. I am of an ancient race. We hunt, we run, we protect: we do not waltz. When you waltz me?—think about it—I am right at member-height.

And now: a walk? A walk?

A walk.

Love,

"Biscuit"

THE GREAT DIVIDER

STAND BACK, MR. DOBBS, LET ME HANDLE THIS

Once upon a time, there was a wealthy country. Just to the south was a poor country. Between them ran a border. People from the poor country were always sneaking over, trying to partake of the wealth of the wealthy country. The people in the wealthy country resented this. Or some did. Some seemed fine with it, and even helped them once they got here. Some said it was a crisis and a big wall was needed. Others said: What crisis? It's been going on for years, plus they work so cheap, you want to pay nine bucks for a freaking quart of strawberries? The national media seized on the story and, as always, screwed it up: reduced it to pithy sound bites, politicized it, and injected it with faux urgency, until, lo, the nation was confused.

Then, a man, a Writer—me, actually—decided to venture forth, to find some answers. Was it a crisis? Was all this excitement justified? Might terrorists someday come in across the border? Was the border really rife with drug-related crime? I went boldly, driving from Brownsville, Texas, to San Diego, California, armed with the ancient tools: objectivity, open-mindedness, a laptop, a rented minivan—a Chrysler Town and Country, to be exact, with electronic everything, including rear and sliding side doors. So as our story unfolds, please imagine these doors periodically sliding/flying open, in the middle of epic Southwestern landscapes, for no reason at all, or simply because I've tried to change the radio station.

GO TO JAIL, AFTER EIGHT TIMES, GO DIRECTLY TO JAIL

In the temporary detention center at the Laredo North Border Patrol Station, a Mexican kid slumps in a chair at a processing desk. He's going to jail for at least three months, because this is the eighth time he's been caught illegally entering the United States, and the system's patience has finally been exhausted.

Border Patrol Agent One runs a hand shyly over his new haircut, which is nearly a buzz.

"That, see, I don't understand that haircut," says Agent Two, wearing a huge cowboy hat.

"At least he's *got* hair," says Agent Three, and Agent Two blushes, acknowledging it: Yes, yes, it's true. Under this hat, I'm bald.

I point to my own head.

We all laugh at my hairline.

Then I look over at the kid. He's sitting there expressionless, a small cat among large dogs. And now he's got to endure this balding talk, this nervous braying laughter, before he can get to the next enjoyable step (being processed), and on to the part where he gets sent off to a foreign jail.

My heart goes out to him.

Sort of.

Because empathy depends on how you've spent your day. I've just spent mine driving around in a "marked caged unit" with Agent Three, aka Dan Garibay: visiting the muddy clearings where illegal aliens change into dry clothes after they cross, inspecting fence-cuts, driving past safe houses, hearing agents talk about tracking groups of illegals for eleven straight hours. I've learned that it's now more profitable to traffic in humans than in drugs; that MS-13, a Salvadoran gang, is in a death struggle with the more traditional Mexican Mafia; that Border Patrol agents in Laredo are routinely shadowed by spies from the smuggling cartels who, in turn, are shadowed by a newly formed countersurveillance unit.

My relation to this Mexican kid, then, is something like that of a plumber's apprentice to a leak.

Dan's third-generation Mexican American, a funny, reasonable guy who seems to be constantly considering and reconsidering the moral implications of his job. He's got nothing against illegal aliens, understands why they do what they do, has compassionate feelings toward them, and seems committed to catching them in a way that keeps them safe and leaves their dignity intact. But the law is the law, and why should those who break the law be privileged over those who've played by the rules?

So I find myself thinking, re this silent (sullen? unrepentant?) kid, this member of *Wascals Who Insist on Trying to Elude My New Friend Dan*: Dude, what did you expect? *Seven times?* Who doesn't learn after seven times? Do you value your freedom so lightly? Do you have a wife, kids? Do you realize you are now going to miss the next three months of their—

Then, imagining that he has kids, who look like little Mexican versions of my kids back when they were toddlers, I (finally) experience a little heart-pang as I flash on what I'd be thinking if I were him: Laugh it up, you balding bastards, I'm dying here, can't you tell I'm a decent person, oh Jesus, please let me go, just this one last time, they're so cute and will never be this age again, please please, I've made a terrible mistake.

And what will you do if we let you go? I ask him in my mind. Will you try to get in here again? Next time, you could be looking at *five years*.

He hesitates, averts his eyes.

Seriously? I say. My God, is it worth it? Are things really that bad where you live?

And he just looks at me, as if to say: Would I keep trying if it didn't make sense to keep trying, if the possible reward didn't justify possibly getting caught? Do I look stupid?

He doesn't look stupid. He looks handsome and sad and ashamed.

But mostly what he looks is: busted.

Busted, and waiting to pay the price.

HUSTLING FOR SCHOOLBOOKS

I cross the bridge into Nuevo Laredo ("the most dangerous city in North America," according to Dan) with an African American long-haul truck driver from Kentucky who's wearing a cowboy hat and a shirt with a flag sewn on the back. For thirteen years now, whenever he drives this route, he's parked on the U.S. side and saved a few bucks by getting a cheap hotel on the Mexican side. He's divorced, but his wife's a good lady: She's kept him on her insurance, she's a nurse, a good nurse, not a slut like most nurses, who like to fuck the young doctors in the rooms where they keep the towels. Do I know about this? Am I aware of this phenomenon?

In the most dangerous city in North America, a guy's getting his shoes shined with an air of 1950s satisfaction, a row of old people are fingering their pants legs on a bench, a toddler's doing a happy skipping dance along the lip of a fountain.

Not so bad, I think, a town like any other—

Do I want a girl? A boy? A boy from Boy's Town?

A young guy's fallen in beside me: Hector.

"No, man, I'm married," I say. "Happily married."

"Isn't it the case!" he says. "When a man goes with another woman, the wife will give him such a . . . how is it called?"

He mimes slapping himself.

"Slap," I say.

"Your woman will gave you such a slop," he says, shaking his head at the memory of the last time his wife gave him a slop.

Hector advises me: Stay in the shopping area. Do not err to the left or right of the bridge. Avoid the police. Two gangs are fighting for the town, each with its own cops. The cops see you have money, they'll plant drugs on you, take your money, possibly kill you.

Times are hard, he tells me, fewer tourists are coming all the time. His daughter just started first grade, but they haven't been able to afford the books yet. He didn't see his family last night, not having the five bucks necessary for the bus ticket to León.

I give him ten bucks.

He accepts with surprise, gratitude, some disappointment maybe: It's too little money, too early in the night.

He tells me nostalgically about the first time he
sneaked into the United States, with his uncle, in 1989,
in a little boat. His dream is to go over again soon and
join his brother in New Orleans, making fifteen dollars
an hour doing post-Katrina work. He knows about the
location of the new checkpoint, on Highway 83, which I
visited with Dan earlier today, and how to circumvent it:
Get dropped off before the checkpoint, walk a couple of
miles around it, get picked up on the other side.

"Not easy," I say.

"Yes, easy," he says.

And even easier if he had an American to help him.
Do I have a car? Is my car parked in Laredo? If I drive
him through the checkpoint, they won't even stop us.

Ha, ha, ha! I think. Hi, Dan! I can explain!

A muscular scowling guy, face heavily tattooed,
strolls past, with henchmen. Hector, distracted/alarmed,
trips on an exposed pipe.

"He doesn't like me," he says. "Because I am with
you, in his area."

His *area*? I think. The street comes alive with creepi-
ness. This is the town that killed its own police chief, on
his first day in office, for pledging to end the drug trade.

"I should probably head back," I say.

"I think so," says Hector.

Soon the bridge is in sight. Suddenly, he's nervous,
abashed.

Maybe I could give him a little something?

I remind him of the ten dollars.

"That was for my children," he says. "I am asking now
for me. So I can buy a hot dog."

Over the next few seconds I (1) am annoyed at his

nerve, (2) castigate myself for being so tight-sphinctered over—what is it, two bucks?—and (3) hand over the money, smiling warmly to hide the fact that (1) and (2) ever occurred to me.

Hector steps away, buys a hot dog from a vendor, disappears down a side street, raising the hot dog in gratitude.

I cross the bridge.

Easy for me, I think. Impossible for you.

Back in the United States, the facades are nicer, the traffic lighter. My nation appears in that moment as a very clean, anxiety-clenched fist, in the grip of which I feel comfortable and happy, and like myself again.

THE ALL-AMERICAN MEXICAN CITY, OR THE ALL-MEXICAN AMERICAN CITY, WHATEVER

Maybe you've heard some variant of the following:

I have nothing against [Mexicans/immigrants/these people], but nowadays you go to [NAME OF CITY] and all you hear is Spanish. It's as if [these people/the Mexicans/ the foreigners] expect [me/us Americans] to [speak Spanish/adapt to THEIR culture/kowtow to THEM!], whereas the burden ought to be on [them/the newcomers/the Mexicans] to ASSIMILATE, right? Someday soon you're going to find whole American cities full of people speaking only Spanish!

Note to speaker of the above: such a city already exists. Welcome to the Friday-night party that is Laredo.

At Shirley Field, Laredo Martin High is kicking the crap out of Carrizo Springs High before a huge hometown crowd that is virtually all Hispanic and dressed in school-color red. The majorettes conclude their bit, march crisply into the stands, per instructions, with swift precise turns, trying not to crack up. A Mexican American princess (UP UP AND AWAY! reads her T-shirt) searches the crowd, rendered confident and in love with the world by virtue of her beauty, assisted in her search by a heavier, less elated girl.

Show of hands, I think: Anybody here can't afford schoolbooks? Ha ha, no way, the crowd roars in my mind, are you joking? We have SUVs and PlayStations and plenty to eat, we roam the earth expecting respect and receiving it, for we are the American Middle Class, and we shall live out the full measure of our days amidst happiness and plenty.

I leave the game early, have dinner at Taco Palenque, a kind of Taco Bell on glamour pills, tonight inexplicably overrun by gorgeous Mexican American women in tight designer jeans, with glittered eyelids and balletic hairstyles à la Princess Leia. As has been the case all night, only Spanish is being spoken, unless English is needed, in which case English is delivered: gladly, genially, and unaccented.

Tonight, America seems like a happy miracle, a Land o' Plenty where a new ethnicity is being created, an ethnicity that transcends the Anglo/Hispanic distinction, and the primary mascot of this ethnicity is Affluence, accompanied by its beautiful sidekicks Civility, Humor, Kindness, and Relative Absence of Fear. Tonight, America seems like the for-centuries-dreamed-of rescuer of the Little Guy, the place that takes a guy like Hector and puts some pounds on him, sets him on his feet, puts a spring in his step, and ends, forever, his flinching hustle for two-dollar hot dogs.

But first he has to get here.

AMONG THE MENNONITES

The east Texas countryside rolls by: ranches, ranches, elaborate memorials for car-accident-killed Mexican American boys, woven into barbed-wire fences, featuring silk roses and, in at least one case, the small plastic figure of a professional wrestler. It's been unusually rainy, and treetops jut eerily up from a temporary lake, in which it seems hobbits should be fishing from little bark boats.

In Roma, the World Birding Center overlooks a small Mexican village, from which I can hear the ringing of someone's old-fashioned phone.

I'm driving from Laredo to Brownsville to meet with some Mennonites who work with the Mexican American poor in the Rio Grande Valley. Many of the poor are, presumably, undocumented immigrants. I'm feeling a little funny about meeting these Mennonites, because I'm not sure I agree with what they do. If there's a law, and they, even inadvertently, help the undocumented circumvent the law, doesn't this just encourage further lawbreaking, which, in turn, reinforces this system of law-circumvention, which, in turn, strengthens the illegal smuggling cartels, thus ratcheting up the cycle of high profits, violence, and chaos that Dan Garibay described?

Egads, I think, I am become Lou Dobbs.

Later that afternoon, I'm standing in a circle of pretty young women, Teach for America workers, at a Mennonite church social in San Juan. It's muddy and sunny, the music's about to start, across the two-lane is a tract-house neighborhood à la Spielberg, nearby is a movable free-range-chicken shed and an organic garden and a donkey named Pierre, rescued from a neglectful owner by the pastor of the church, John Garland.

John looks more like a guitarist in an indie-rock band than he does a pastor, and his wife, Abby, looks more like the beautiful vocalist in that band than she does a high-school teacher/pastor's wife. John has started a model organic farm here at the church. The idea is to help under-privileged workers access the "intellectual capital" of their work; immigrants are often expert organic farmers who, if they happen to be undocumented, get stuck working for other people, underpaid, or cheated of their pay.

Around them, John and Abby have gathered a group of similarly well-educated, young, politically engaged volunteers working with the poor in small towns across the Rio Grande Valley.

What have they seen?

You name it: blond Spanish-only speakers; mothers who call the school to say they've been deported but will be sneaking back in time for parent-teacher conferences; families in which the kids speak only English and the parents speak only Spanish; families in which the parents speak English but the kids—recent arrivals—can't; kids who came over illegally as babies and are now fully acculturated American teenagers—excellent straight-A students who, because they're undocumented, can't get financial aid for college, which means, given their family economics, no college for them at all.

So what do they do?

"They go to work," Abby says.

John has told me that although their mission involves "reaching out to those in need"—some of whom, in this area especially, may indeed be undocumented—they don't have a clue if people have documents or not. Still, remembering my Lou Dobbs moment, I ask John and Abby if they ever have doubts about working with the undocumented, since technically it's against the law.

John looks at me thoughtfully from behind his glasses.

"Absolutely," he says. "Just the other day, these two guys walked up here and said, 'Hey, man, we just crossed the river, we're really thirsty, we need some water.' And I looked them over and said: 'Sorry, friend, you'll have to take it up the road.'"

Abby nods.

So this is interesting. They are, yes, Christians, and yet they understand that the law forbids—

Then they both crack up.

"Yeah, see that big cross on the front of the church?" says Abby. "That's actually what it means: Take it up the road."

"The thing is, when you read the Bible?" John says. "One thing it's not is wishy-washy about our responsibility toward people in need. Yes, there's the law, and we should respect it, but there's also a higher law."

In Abby's opinion, the problem with this immigration debate is the level of abstraction at which it's conducted. If you talk about *undocumented workers* or *illegal aliens*, it's easy to make mistakes. Whereas if you say: *This is Valerie, Valerie is my student, whom I love,* then whatever you do will make sense, coming, as it does, from the heart, with a real person in mind.

A STORY TOO SAD TO INVENT

Because of the way Lupe Aguilar's past has been described to me, I expect him to be mean and wiry and street-scarred, but no: He's white-haired, gentle, and articulate, with a quality of patient abiding that makes me instantly crave his approval. After church, at the head of a long familial table in a Mexican restaurant, he tells me he used to: (1) run wild (his wife's sitting across the table, and her eyebrows go up, indicating: Oh *yes* he did), (2) shepherd groups of recently arrived Mexicans into a hotel room, take his fee, then rat them out to the Border Patrol, (3) own bars, party, and fight (a guy he offended once put three slugs in his back). Then he experienced a religious conversion and is now a Mennonite pastor who shelters the homeless—in his house, in trailers behind his house, in the kitchen of his church (as we enter, a smiling, timid family just arrived from Veracruz rises as one, exclaims *mucho gusto* as one, sits as one), or in the church itself (in the Sunday-school rooms, in the sanctuary, beside the altar), with a disregard for his personal space that I find impossible to imagine. Would I let strangers sleep in my home, at my work, would I let a constant flow of Unknown Quantities stream past my kids?

No, I would not.

And this isn't just my paranoia; Lupe says people he's helped have stolen from him (he's lost three cars this way), insulted him, made indecent proposals to his wife and daughters. He's not a big favorite of the neighbors, either, some of whom consider him a lawbreaker. But he feels doing this work is his duty. Once, back in his early days as a Christian, a young Mennonite volunteer overheard him use the word *wetback* and referred him to Matthew 25:40 ("Whatever you did for one of the least of these brothers of mine, you did for me"). Reading this, Lupe says, he was "changed forever." His goal in life is now "to be humble and meek like Jesus," and you see this desire working through him, in the things he does and the way he attempts to deflect credit ("Jesus is the doer!").

To illustrate the way the current system of illegality creates secrecy and chaos, which in turn brings down worlds of shit, mostly on the poor, he tells me the following story:

Once upon a time, a young couple left Mexico and came north. Trying to avoid the Border Patrol, they crossed the river in a remote area, where they were set upon by "border bandits" who stole their shoes and money and raped the woman in front of the man. She became pregnant. Having become Christians, and after much soul-searching, the couple decided to keep the baby. But the woman's water broke at five months, and the baby died ten minutes after its birth. The couple couldn't afford a coffin, so Lupe called in a favor from a funeral director; the funeral home allowed a brief (twenty-minute) ceremony and donated a small cardboard box for the burial. The Mennonites acquired a small plot from the county and drove out in their own cars to bury the baby. At the grave, Lupe had to pry the dead baby out of the grieving mother's arms. The woman was a mess but, being undocumented, was too afraid to seek psychological help. In her heart, she blamed the man for not defending her, blamed herself for not being able to carry the baby to full-term, blamed God for not helping them. The man, for his part, couldn't make peace with the way he'd failed to protect her. In the end, the pain proved too much, and the couple separated.

The end.

"WHAT DO WE WANT? DEPORT THEM NOW!"

Let's meet the *Rodriguezes*, who came from a *Very Poor Central American Country* and now live in *Somewhere, Texas*.

The Rodriguez males are legal, the females not. Mr. Rodriguez came illegally but has since gotten his paperwork in order; their baby son was born here and so is a citizen— but the wife and daughters remain undocumented.

I visit them in their home, which Mr. Rodriguez built, by hand, out of cinder blocks, over the past five years, when not working his first job (laying tile), his second (factory watchman), or his third (growing their food in a backyard garden). The gray cinder blocks, arched doorways, and poured-concrete floor give the house the feeling of a medieval castle, had the king driven masonry nails into the cinder block in order to hang some framed family photos.

To get here, Mr. R. worked his way north through Mexico for two years, doing construction, learning local dialects along the way to avoid getting busted by Mexican immigration. He's a big guy, hearty and happy, somebody you'd see beaming down from a Diego Rivera mural, but his time on the road seems to have spooked him. He saw people shaken down, unfairly arrested, robbed, murdered. He saw "lots of lifeless bodies" along the road.

"The real horror," he says, "was in Mexico."

For two years, his wife didn't hear from him.

How did she feel during this silence?

She suddenly looks physically sick, says she doesn't like to think of that time, when she was sure he was dead. She was trying to keep the farm going, baking *pan dulce* in a mud oven he'd built, a hundred small loaves at a time. Twice a week, she'd walk into town, tray on her head, and in this way supported a family of five.

Then came the earthquake.

It ruptured the walls of their adobe house, and she moved herself and the children into a shed she built of three sheets of government-supplied sheet metal, which was just big enough for a bed and a table, and unbearably hot in the daytime.

Then, one day, a letter came from America. He'd crossed on an inner tube, in a group, with coyote help, and lived briefly in a safe house that he left as soon as he found it was also being used in the drug trade.

"Wow," I say, "how did you feel when you first saw his handwriting—"

"*Muy contenta*, she says, with a smile so spontaneous and uncontrived you'd think their two-year separation had just that instant ended.

They don't have insurance, she says, but then again, they never get sick: All their food is fresh, from their garden, she breast-fed the babies, they get good milk and cheese from their goats. In the past, she's tried government-sponsored health-care programs, but she felt kind of ashamed accepting government aid and probably won't be doing it again.

"It's nice remembering these things," he says, "now that we are all here together. But also it's sad, because I remember those left behind on the road."

"What's your dream?" I ask. "You know, your eventual dream for your—"

"I have arrived at my dream already," he says.

The oldest daughter brings in some vegetables from their garden—okra, big fat peppers. Is she, the daughter, in school?

"I'm a junior," she says in perfect English.

Her passion is math. She wants to be a math teacher. I mention that my daughter's in the throes of quadratic equations.

"Oh," she says shyly. "I love those."

"You love quadratic equations," I say.

"I *love* them," she says.

If this isn't the essential American story, I don't know what is: Guy hews a life out of nothing, by working every waking moment, with no education, no government help, no external advantages whatsoever, and no ulterior motive. What did he want? A place where his kids could grow up, with less fear and more material comforts.

Did he get it?

Yes, he did, God bless him.

LET US REDUCE OUR ENEMIES, SO WE CAN MOCK THEM MORE EASILY

The Minuteman Project is kicking off Operation Sovereignty, their "largest operation to date," with a rally on a narrow strip-mall berm in Laredo. It's a rally in the modern-American style: participants few, Media many.

The Minutemen angrily shout, "What do we want? Deport them now!"

Members of the Unión de Trabajadores del Suroeste angrily shout, "Hey ho, hey ho, racist Minutemen got to go!"

A jaunty Mexican American, in wraparound sunglasses, wearing a serape, waving a Mexican flag, angrily shouts, "Who picks your potatoes? Who builds your houses?"

A Minuteman angrily shouts, re the Mexican Flag Guy, "He told me to get out of his CITY! This is my COUNTRY, man!"

Everyone's pissed, oppositional, less empathetic and articulate and well-mannered than they would be at any other moment in their actual lives. The Media rushes around, sticking their cameras into the face of whoever's behaving most badly at the moment.

A bespectacled little dude in a huge cowboy hat says he's running for Congress in Austin.

"How's it going?" I ask.

"Bad," he says. "I don't have any money."

Does he have a position on the immigration issue? He does: Borders make a country, and we need a better border, namely, a wall.

But how do you do that, just, you know, physically?

Simple. Alter the border. Cede land to Mexico until the border is a long, straight line. Then run your wall from here to California.

I imagine that ugly map, beautiful border-curves of the Rio Grande made computer-straight.

I step over for a word with the Mexican Flag Guy. Because of my appearance (white, baseball-capped, middle-aged), he mistakes me for a Minuteman until, to prove I'm not a Minuteman, I disparage the Minutemen. We're walking by a light pole, the base of which is exposed, a Possible Tripping Hazard. He points it out, saying that had I been a Minuteman, he would've let me fall on my ass.

Nearby, three Minutewomen stand in the midday sun with a sign: *Mexico's a Bad Neighbor.*

The Mexican Flag Guy taunts them: "It's hot in that sun, isn't it? That's what you like about us, right? We don't burn, baby!"

Which is kind of weird, since two of the Minutewomen are Hispanic, presumptive fellow nonburners.

Here's the story of how one of these women, Lupe Moreno, became a Minutewoman:

As a teenager, her son had a car accident and ended up partially paralyzed. In the next hospital bed was an illegal who'd broken his arm coming over the wall. Once treated, he ran away. After Lupe's son was released, she started getting nagging letters from the hospital, demanding the hundred-dollar copay. She found this infuriating: This illegal gets thousands of dollars of treatment free, and they're nagging *her*? To make matters worse, her son needed a wheelchair but could only have one free for the first week of his stay. Through her work in social services, Lupe was aware of a special program through which, had her son been illegal, he could have gotten a wheelchair free and kept it indefinitely.

"You mean 'undocumented,'" I say.

"I call them illegals," she says, "because that's what they are."

GENTLE DIGNIFIED MAN 1,
MINUTEMEN 0

A cluster of Minutemen are shouting across the berm-defining shrub at a sixtysomething Mexican American in a VIETNAM baseball cap: If he DID fight for this country, as implied by his cap, why isn't he willing to fight for it NOW, by protecting it from illegal inVADers?

He fires back: "I was fighting for this country when you were in Pampers, brother!"

This country kicked the black man around for hundreds of years, he shouts, and now that the black man has finally stood up for himself, the country's looking for someone new to kick, and its eyes have fallen on the brown man, but the brown man built this country, always working cheap, and is not about to become the whipping boy, no sir, not at this late stage of the game.

The uncontrived passion in his voice is shutting the Minutemen down, but then the Unión de Trabajadores del Suroeste people start inadvertently drowning him out with their ("RACIST MINUTEMEN GOT TO—") bullhorns.

A certain Writer, behaving unprofessionally, sneaks over, tells the bullhorn guys to hold off: This Vietnam guy is really kicking ass.

A Unión de Trabajadores del Suroeste guy rushes a bullhorn to the Vietnam guy, and soon the Minutemen, discouraged, have drifted away to a distant part of the berm.

"We're farmers, you know?" a friend of the Vietnam guy tells me. "Born and raised here in Laredo. We've worked hard all our lives. All of this, all this anger, all this aggression . . ." And he waves his hand wearily at what's left of the rally. "What I think is, we're here on this earth to take care of one another."

IN WHICH I AM CHOKED

I get a few minutes with Jim Gilchrist, founder of the Minuteman Project.

What I want to ask is, Why are you guys so mad about everything? Why so scared? Where's the love?

Instead I say, "I've read that you're a Christian. What's the relation of this Minuteman ethic to your Christianity?"

"Charity is good," he says. "Benevolence is good. But charity begins at home. And their home is Mexico."

Gilchrist is a likable guy in his fifties who reminds me of the actor who played the mayor in *Jaws*. He speaks in meandering Stengelese paragraphs; your mind struggles to summarize them, but they will not yield. Strong passions, about something or other, keep emitting forth from him, in a sideways manner that makes you keep listening, in the same way that seeing a beginner skater fly by carrying a stack of dishes might make you keep watching. He's always saying things like "I've got him in my crosshairs!" or "He's OK for now, he hasn't crossed me yet, he's making all the right noises!" or (of the late Steve Irwin): "He was probably one of these open-border cranks, but I give him a pass—I liked his show," or (of an African American Minuteman in Los Angeles, with admiring glee): "That guy just burned an effigy of Osama bin Laden—in front of a mosque!"

Gilchrist can be seen on YouTube, saying, of a crowd of chanting protesters at Ground Zero, "This is not the first time I've faced Satan. . . . This will not be the last time," but in person he's gentlemanly, timid almost. This is communicated via something in his listening posture: leaning slightly forward, a kind of wincing going on around the eyes.

After the rally, the Minutepeople convoy out to Eagle Pass, where the Op will begin in earnest. We stop at a convenience store to fuel up. Trying to engage Gilchrist, I roll down the van window, jocularly tell him smoking's a nasty habit.

"Well," he says, "I don't do drugs, I don't drink much . . . and I've recently given up ATTEMPTED MURDER!"

At the words *attempted murder*, putting a mock-crazy expression on his face, he reaches in through the van window and fake-throttles me around the neck.

I have no problem with this. I'm from Chicago. Chicago males often bond via fake kicks to the groin. So I feel I'm getting off easy.

Although I also think: (1) Wow, that was a pretty energetic fake-choke, and (2) Has this guy not undergone media training?

We drive two hours into the country, looking for

illegals along the way—in particular, it would seem, for illegals too deaf or stupid to hide when they hear a twelve-car convoy approaching.

NO, TELL ME WHAT YOU REALLY THINK

Here are some facts about Minutepeople, or at least the eight I had dinner with that night, at Skillet's Restaurant in Eagle Pass, Texas:

Minutepeople are fun. You can't insult them. They're willing to entertain any point of view. They like to debate. They look stern at first, do a lot of scowling, but behind their eyes, once you get them talking, there's a hurt, docile quality, possibly related to past wrongs done them, a quality I associate with the thunked-as-kids: Long ago the world turned on them in some unexpected and unpleasant way, and they are, not unreasonably, expecting that it could happen again at any moment. The Barney-Fifish quality of their bluster recedes immediately upon challenge, and they go soft, and you somehow magically become Dad.

I announce myself as an Eastern Liberal, and am thereafter treated like a minicelebrity or lab specimen, a living example of a rare species they've heretofore only heard about on Fox. Paradoxically, my opinions seem to matter to them. They're oddly deferential. They listen. When I argue that, despite our gun laws, Manhattan is safer than Houston, or assert that, yes, there are working-class people in New York City, they take me on faith, adjust their arguments accordingly, and seem happy for the correction, because it means I was taking their argument seriously in the first place.

I ask if Minutemen ever bring guns on their Ops.

"We all have guns," someone says.

"We all have guns *here*," says someone else.

"This is Texas," says a third someone. "Totally legal."

Their guns, in fact, are influencing their choice of hotels: They have to be able to bring their weapons inside.

"The thing about people from New York?" says Shannon, founder of the Texas Minutemen, who has been smiling at me in passing all day in a way that manages to be suspicious, deferential, and welcoming all at once. "Is they're rude."

"It's the way they talk to you," someone else says.

Has he, Shannon, ever been to New York?

"Haw haw! Yeah, right!" says Shannon. "Like I'm going to that crazy place without my guns."

They honestly don't go anywhere they can't bring their guns?

Nope. The world is too insane. It would be irresponsible to put themselves at that kind of risk.

Chicago?

Haw.

Boston?

Please.

How about Mexico? Have they ever been over there?

The most enthusiastic guffaws yet. Am I kidding? The cartels, they say, have a bounty out on them: twenty-five grand for any Minuteman. And for Shannon: fifty grand.

"Shannon's a star," someone says.

Being called a star seems to rev Shannon up. He takes the floor, presents a discourse that might be entitled: "My Thoughts on Bitches."

He has a friend who once lived with two lesbians and

slept with them both, together and separately. However, problems developed when this friend, unwisely, "started hitting one harder than the other." Shannon has to admit it: Girlwise, the only thing he really likes? Is dominating them.

There was this one gal, for example, who kept being uncooperative. Finally, she, kind of uncooperatively, more or less cooperated. To celebrate his victory, he stole her bra, then hung it from his car antenna. There's nothing like it, he says, like dominating them. Then he emits a phrase so crude, so poetically dense—it combines images of (1) a small furry beast and (2) two swinging-down thingies—that I want to get out my notebook and ask him to repeat it, but I chicken out, and the exact wording is lost forever, but suffice to say: What made that particular furry beast/swinging thingy combo so delightful to Shannon was that, although towering over Shannon, it had consented to be dominated by him.

Ah, but that's all in the past, he sighs. Of late he's gotten "some sane wisdom." He knows what he looks like. These days if a woman says she finds him attractive, he just asks how much it's going to cost him. Or he looks behind him to determine who she's really talking to.

This makes me sad. Under the bluster, he seems like a nice guy, a gentle guy, even, a doting husband waiting to happen, possibly, capable of loving and being loved in return. If only he could just—

Wait, wait, I think, why are you being such a sucker? Did he or did he not just say the things he just said? Stop trying so hard to be Johnny Compassion. Why is he talking such rude shit?

I turn to Lesley, the lone Minutewoman at the table.

"Is this guy a misogynist or what?" I say. "You don't find this offensive?"

"I'm not easily intimidated," she says, laughing. "Do I look like I'm easily intimidated?"

Some National Guardsmen come in and sit nearby, and this gets us on the subject of Iraq. Brian, a smart, articulate Minuteman, originally from Massachusetts, who has traveled all over the world—Brazil, Japan, India—says Fallujah should have been leveled. He sends this out like a blustering trial balloon. Is he nuts? I ask. How many women and children would that have required killing? Well, he says, that happens once, it doesn't happen again. Hello? I say. Are you really saying that? Little kids, old ladies? Well, he says, you order them out first. Come on, I say, think about New Orleans. People in Fallujah are much poorer than that, how do they "get out"? What do they do, rent cars? Call taxis? Could you give that order? I don't think you could, and I don't think you would.

He looks chastened and does a remarkable thing, given that he's arguing with a Liberal, in front of his people: He reverses position.

"You're right," he says. "I wouldn't, no."

Through it all, our Mexican American waitress, resembling a pretty Delhi street waif courtesy of her thick mascara, comes and goes, being spoken gently to by Shannon and the others, in the courteous quasi-military tones favored by the Minutepeople.

LOST PATROL THAT CAN'T SHOOT STRAIGHT FAILS TO FIND ASS WITH BOTH HANDS

Next morning we "go out on recon," meaning we walk around the ranch we'll be guarding later tonight.

An upbeat guy named Curtis, president of U.S. Border Watch, leads us Media around, pointing out evidence of illegals (a tamped-down human-size nest in some reeds, a fence-cut, some garbage) and marking several "possible deployment spots" using bits of a cow skull he's found: The white bone will be visible later in the moonlight. An irrigation ditch running parallel to the border is a plus; the sound of the illegals wading the ditch will serve as a kind of early-warning system.

We walk the fence line. The neighboring rancher isn't on board, so the Op will be confined to about a three-hundred-yard stretch of this ranch.

"We're in a real rat race here," Curtis says on his cell, as we start back to the cars. "The Media's pounding us."

We Media look around, puzzled. We're not pounding anybody. We're just walking quietly behind Curtis, having our little Media thoughts.

We take a shortcut back through a grove of mesquite. Shannon says this reminds him of a forest near the Knights of Pythias home where he was sent to live during his parents' divorce. Soon it becomes clear we're lost. The cars can't be more than a hundred yards away, but we don't seem to be getting any closer. Curtis suggests somebody send a radio message to base camp, i.e., the cars, see if somebody can honk a horn or something.

Radio contact proves problematic.

From the front of the group, some grumbling: Ahead is a creek. There's much concern, shouted optimization instructions, extended hands, some awkward scrambling up the opposite muddy slope, good-humored postcrossing comparisons of soaked pants legs, Media and Minutepersons united as one.

Then the group bunches up. Again, a surprise: There's a barbed-wire fence ahead, literally five feet from the lip of the creek, and as the front of the group struggles through the fence (coats snagging on barbed wire, on mesquite branches, raindrops plopping off trees), a cry goes up: Jeez, another fence!

Besides this one?

Yes, yes, a whole other fence.

We are, like, caught between these two improbably close-together, nonparallel fences, in a forest no cow could ever enter. How odd. What a perverse rancher.

"Makes you kind of respect the illegals," a Minute-person says sweetly.

Suddenly: shouts of consternation from the front of the group, which has freed itself from the two-fence trap, only to find—

"What you got?" Curtis shouts.

It appears there is a second creek, which may even qualify as a small, deep river, beyond this second fence, which is proving even stouter and more gnarly than the first. Jesus, where the hell are we? Who designed this freaking ranch, Escher?

"I thought all y'all media were supposed to be neutral," smirks Shannon. "Not so neutral now, are you?"

This is so nutty as to be hilarious.

"We're being neutral," I say. "By not making fun of you."

"Attention all units!" Curtis cries out, to those of us still on this side of River Two. "If you have not crossed the ravine yet, do not cross! I repeat, do not cross!"

I can see the headline now, if anyone escapes to write it: "Minutemen Die of Starvation in Tiny Thicket, Comically Close to Own Cars."

A photographer with bad knees goes down, is lifted to his feet by Brian, the guy who last night advocated the annihilation of Fallujah, whose face, as he goes to the photographer's aid, is transformed by a look of sudden radiant concern.

In time, as in a beautiful dream, we arrive back at the cars. Is our leadership crushed, humiliated, bitterly angry, ordering us not to tell anyone? On the contrary. Our leaders are cheerful, triumphant, hyped with victory, as if this Getting Lost never happened, or maybe as if, having been closely involved with embarrassing debacles all their lives, they have learned an excellent coping strategy: deny, smile, move on.

Through my mind runs the phrase: *Shows Good Spirit*.

WITH GUNS IT IS NOT SO FUNNY

At dusk, the same Good-Spirited crew that nearly met its doom in the Land of Infinite Fences arrives back at the ranch, heavily armed. We Media are kind of shocked into silence at the extent of the armament. Every Minuteman's got at least a shotgun, a rifle, or a machine-gun-looking semiautomatic weapon. My Team Leader, Art (a fearsome biker-looking dude, six-one, 250, shaved-headed, bearded, tattooed, who is, in fact, a biker but is also a troubleshooter for a fiber-optic network and a member of Mensa), has, in addition to his semiautomatic: a .45 down each pants leg, a long, jagged knife he calls his "Arkansas toothpick," and a two-shot Derringer designed to fire shotgun shells.

I tell him that because I'm a Liberal and he's so large, I expect that, if there's trouble, he will carry me to safety.

He gives me a look I would describe as: the *ornery-eye-twinkle-of-possible-friendship*, reminding me of my childhood friend K., who was equally happy explicating *The Art of War* or driving his head through a wall.

Darkness falls; the moon comes up. Our Team advances into the brush. Through a kind of willful mass hypnosis, aided by all this wishful costuming, things suddenly go very Vietnam, and a tense, watchful quiet falls over the group.

It's scary—partly because we're making it scary and partly because (1) real illegals really do cross here, led by real members of the real smuggling cartels, and (2) these are real guns.

Suddenly, weirdly, I find my eyes tearing up: How many times, through the long centuries of life on earth, has one group of men sneaked armed into the woods, hoping to surprise a second group not expecting them? And where has this gotten us? I feel sad for whomever we might catch (some little family even now timidly approaching in the dark?) and sad for the Minutemen, plodding forward like ghosts doomed to hunt That Which Causes Them Anxiety through all eternity.

We spread out in the dark, three teams of three Minutepeople each, about a hundred yards between each group.

This is the total extent of Operation Sovereignty: nine guys, four Media, along a few hundred yards of border, on one small ranch, in the huge state of Texas.

A tiny patch of Catcher in a thousand miles of Rye.

OUR TEAM MAY SURPRISE YOU

Our Team takes up its position: in some long grass, besieged by bugs. I wish we could sit over there, on that less buggish dirt road, but Art has positioned us here, and something in me is cheerfully rising to the faux-military discipline.

Soon the sky is crossed with parallel rivers of low milky stars.

Scott's from Houston, the founder of the Texas Militia. He's just out here getting some experience points, he says. This is his first Op, he can only stay a week; what with work (graphic design) and his Militia stuff (four membership applications at home waiting to be processed), he's superbusy. Plus, of course, he's got RenFaire coming up—

"RenFaire?" I say.

"Renaissance Faire," he says.

"Do you . . . You do that?" I say.

He does. He does the whole deal. He's got a twelve-hundred-dollar suit of leather armor, does an English accent but, no, has not developed a role-play, seeing as how he is merely a Playtron, and Playtrons are not paid to interact with patrons, i.e., Mundanes.

Our third Team Member, Lance, so far known to me only as an angry, frustrated voice piping up now and then to express a sense that everything is all fucked up and being orchestrated by sinister forces from far away, is sitting under a tree. I join him there, out of the moonlight, in what, in daytime, would be shade.

He recently married a Russian woman he met online, he says. For many years, he says, he was a—

The next bit is unintelligible. Or impossible. I ask him to repeat.

No, I've heard right: For many years he was a dancer with the Houston Ballet.

"Of course, you wouldn't know it to look at me now," he says.

He and his wife appeared on a Ricki Lake segment on Russian mail-order brides. He didn't do what so many guys seeking Russian brides do, he says, i.e., go to a mass meet-and-greet in some St. Petersburg hotel; his wife is from a small town, and he went there to meet her, and they really connected, from the heart. She's a great lady, and they're so happy together, she's just—he shakes his head, not quite believing his good fortune.

When he talks about his wife, the paranoiac quality of his political discourse drops away, and he becomes relaxed and confident. He owns a construction company but is thinking of doing something different with his life, making some investments. He's thinking, in fact, of buying the RenFaire in Houston.

I'm a little confused. Does he know . . . Does he know that Scott also is involved with RenFaire?

"Sure, that's how we met," he says. "Scott's in the Torturers' Guild."

We wait and wait for some Mexicans to blunder over the border and plop into the irrigation ditch.

But nobody comes.

NEARLY THE DEATH OF SOME GUY NAMED CARL

Waiting implies an eventual end to waiting, which produces dramatic structure.

Somebody radios: Team Two, a car is approaching your position.

A car is indeed approaching. Art's whispering on the radio: Is it one of ours? Is it? Anybody read me?

No answer.

"You Media, take cover around the corner," he says. The corner is, like, behind those trees, ten feet away.

I take cover by walking over, standing there, feeling a little stupid.

Scott drops to one knee, raises his shotgun. Lance goes down on his belly, sights down the barrel of his semiautomatic. Our Team suddenly looks like a Baghdad checkpoint.

I'm thinking: Hold on now, isn't this probably a rancher, a lost rancher, a lost tipsy guest of a rancher?

The car—a white Oldsmobile—appears, slowly, slowly, just the way a drug smuggler or cartel pickup car would.

It seems to pause as it passes.

Somebody hisses: He just— Did he just drop something? Lance and Scott rush forward to have a look at the dropped thing. What is it? Drugs? A bag of, uh, narcotics?

Negative, it's just a plastic bag they hadn't noticed before.

A call comes from Team One, down the line: The vehicle was Carl. This makes us, Team Two, very angry. That stupid Carl! Why the hell didn't Carl radio? Who is Carl, anyway? How many Ops has he done? Scott barks: "Carl better pull head out of rear, or next time he's going to get his car filled with lead!"

"No, no," Art says. "No free fire permitted, don't get all—"

The Minutemen cannot detain an illegal. They cannot harass. All they can do is call the Border Patrol. So why the guns? They don't, they say, want to be overrun by the cartel. Has a Minuteman ever been shot, or shot at, by the cartel? No. But conceptualizing the cartel dudes as Scarfacian monsters, the Minutemen come out armed to meet them in the night and thereby rev themselves up, and yet there's no training—Art is the most experienced Minuteman on our Team (Lance and Scott are both first-timers).

So, a prediction: Eventually, somebody's going to get shot. It may be a Minuteman, it may be a cartel dude, it may be some little kid standing scared at the back of a group of migrants—but eventually, I tell Art, all this tension and drama is going to lead to something tragic.

"You don't come into my house, man," Art says.

"This isn't your house," I say.

"Oh, it sure is," he says. "This is my country."

"Your house is your house," I say. "This is some dude's ranch."

IF ONLY THERE WERE MICROWAVE POPCORN

Boredom sets in. Our Team talks.

Boy, do we.

At times, they're so Right and I'm so Left, we agree. I say I don't like big agribusiness. They agree. We agree that NAFTA stinks, but for different reasons: I say it disadvantages the small Mexican farmer; they say it presages a European Union–style mega-nation. They, like me, are not fans of President Bush (who called the Minutemen "vigilantes"), but they, like me, do like Jon Stewart.

They do *not* like: George Soros; La Raza; signs in Spanish; the term *Hispanic*; the term *African American* ("I'm not an Irish-American, I'm an AMERICAN"); the federal government (which, they claim, routinely provides the Mexican government info on the time and place of their Ops); the fact that the Mexican Flag Guy at the rally was holding the Mexican flag higher than the American flag; being compelled to accommodate anyone, in any way ("I don't mind being compassionate," says Art,

"but I don't want you to *force* me to be compassionate");
and the dull conformity of the American masses ("Most
people are sheep," says Art. "They're sheeple. The guys
you meet out here? Are at least trying to get out of the
sheepskins.").

A civil war's coming within the next four years, they
say: The warring parties will include the police and the
government/corporate coalition and the Mexicans and
the people like them, the non-sheeples, for whom the
government is, even as we speak, preparing secret concentration camps.

We go on and on, because we're bored and because,
turns out, we all belong to the same species: the American
Male Opinionated Chatterbox.

Around midnight a tough-looking guy with a ban-
dage across his nose, a former Air Force sergeant everyone's been, not surprisingly, referring to as Sarge,
comes stomping over. "What *is* this?" he barks. "A prayer
meeting?"

The Team freezes, suddenly identified as: Yappy Fems
Who Talk Too Much.

"We're talking too quiet for God to hear us," says
Lance.

"God always hears us, man," says Art solemnly.

Sarge stomps off, spends the rest of the night sitting
by the irrigation ditch like a bitter mystic. We continue
to enthusiastically surmise, theorize, construct alter-
native governmental models, occasionally crack up; we
start at a respectful whisper and gradually modulate
up to kegger-level roaring. If there were any Mexicans
in the vicinity that night, I expect they mistook us for a
New Age sleepover, went down the road a few ranches,
and crossed there.

HAVING STEMMED THE TIDE OF INVADING ILLEGALS, WE RETIRE FOR THE EVENING

We're tired. Art's face, earlier lean and savage, begins to kind of melt, increasing in affability and weariness, until finally he makes the call: Knees and legs are going here, maybe we should live to fight another day, tomorrow let's remember the lawn chairs.

We quit at three, slog back to the cars.

"Ready to debrief, sir!" shouts our sole black Minuteman, Booker, who then shines his flashlight on Brian, who's got a tricked-out AR-15 with a SureFire sighting module. Booker's tongue drops out of his mouth, and he starts moaning and thrashing his head around.

"Dude, what are you doing?" says Brian.

"I just had an orgasm," says Booker.

Curtis gathers us around.

All in all, he feels, it went well. He was impressed with the professionalism exhibited here tonight. These media people didn't see a single white racist KKK person out here tonight, he doesn't believe.

"That's right," says Booker. "They haven't hung me up yet!"

WELL, NOT ALL OF US RETIRE

I can't find a room in Eagle Pass, so just start driving. I make it nearly to Del Rio, start falling asleep at the wheel, then park the minivan in a white-stone quarry, get out to pee.

Mounted on a pile of drill pipe is the severed head of a buck.

Around the head, five does pay tribute.

At the sound of my many electronic doors flying/sliding open at once, the mounted head grows a body, then disappears up a steep cliff, followed by its worshipful does.

It occurs to me I'm too tired to be driving.

I sleep a few hours, drive west all morning. I pass a vulture feeding on a baby deer, then another vulture feeding on a second baby deer, then a third vulture feeding on a small unrecognizable thing, decide to discontinue the noting of vulture sightings.

Then it's Big Bend National Park, like a Pecos Bill cartoon. Cacti, dust devils, a couple of mules preparing to fuck, the horizon a kind of Model Showroom for Used Mountains: Here's something kind of Gibraltar, if you like that; a huge cleft chin; a classic butte; a Tibetan hooked-nose cliff; four in a row we just got in from Peru (see how they're covered with green near their peaks?); a flattop; a Rushmorish one with faces in it, but not the faces of anybody famous.

Above the Used Mountains appear three Muppet-looking clouds, the size you imagine God to be when you're a kid and imagine God has size.

The countryside is so big, so gorgeous, that it outs human ideas for what they are: inventions, projections, approximations, delusions. In the face of all this Size, action seems pathetic and comic, and fearful, preemptive action seems most pathetic and comic of all.

I find I've been made sad by Minuteman dread. They take a fact and make the worst of it. This beautiful world, all this magnificence, seems to inspire in them only a fear that the beautiful world will be taken away. I liked them, I had a good time with them, but it feels good to be away from them, out in all this open space, where anything could be true, and what is true might even be good.

A PLACE WHERE WHAT IS TRUE IS
AT THE VERY LEAST BEING MADE
A LITTLE BETTER

In the old days, the border crossing at Rio Grande Village was considered a Category B, or "historical," crossing. Mexicans from Boquillas would cross by rowboat to shop at the little American grocery, and it was considered part of "the Big Bend experience" for American tourists to cross into Boquillas and spend the day there.

But a few months after September 11, a TV helicopter shot some footage of a couple of guys wading across, and Boquillas was identified as an example of Appallingly Porous Border Syndrome. On May 10, 2002, the crossing was closed, as were those at two nearby villages, Paso Lajitas and Santa Elena.

The effect of these closings has been the slow death of the villages. Boquillas has shrunk from 250 to 90 people. The store, denied its Mexican shoppers, has lost 40 percent of its business. Paso Lajitas is made up mostly of people too old to relocate and who have to drive eleven miles on a terrible dirt road to get their drinking water. Santa Elena is now down to just three families.

I hear about this from Cynta de Narvaez, a former Manhattan debutante, Studio 54 vet, crew chief for the French hot-air balloon team, and river guide, as we sit on her porch in Terlingua.

Imagine a map, Cynta says. Color drug activity purple. Before the closures, you would have seen a few blips. Now the entire fucking border is purple. Stop watering half a plant; parasites move into the dry half, it dies.

The Terlingua hippies used to take their town band, Los Pinche Gringos (the Freaking Gringos), over to Paso Lajitas on weekend nights for a binational all-ages hoedown: grandmothers dancing with nine-year-old boys, fathers dancing with babies in their arms. But this is now a five-hour trip for the Americans; they can still cross at Lajitas but legally have to come back in via the Customs Station at Ojinaga.

So no more dance parties.

"This was a bicultural community before they closed the border," she says. "The people over there aren't numbers, they have names and faces. We've danced together, reached for onions in the store at the same time."

But the hippies struck back.

So far they've sent a solar-powered water pump and two wind-powered generators across to Boquillas, begun facilitating a craft-importing business for the Boquillans, bought a solar water pump for Paso Lajitas, and are working on one for San Vincente, which, in the meantime, is being served by a Terlingua-provided reverse-osmosis water filter.

"At least they know we haven't forgotten them," Cynta says. "And they know we're not our government. Love thy neighbor, right? Not only does it give you the warm fuzzies, you get to live in the world without worrying."

Cynta's been sick, with Lyme disease. Her adrenals are all but gone. She recently, briefly, lost the use of her arms.

But she's feeling pretty good today.

The mind, it occurs to me, is an engine. There is an ambient mode in which the mind sits idling, before there is information. Some minds idle in a kind of dreading crouch, waiting to be offended. Others stand up straight, eyes slightly wide, expecting to be pleasantly surprised. Some minds, imagining the great What Is Out There, imagine it intends doom for them; others imagine there is something out there that may be suffering and in need of their help.

Which is right?

Neither.

Both.

Maybe all of our politics is simply neurology writ large. Maybe there are a finite number of idling modes. Maybe there are just two broad modes, and out of this fact comes our current division.

I'M READY FOR MY CLOSE-UP, MR. YOAKAM

In certain places, the border possesses a lovely kid's-book geometry. For example: Per my map, there should be *an exact spot* where the border stops being the Rio Grande and starts being a fence.

And there is. It's behind a brick works near El Paso.

Standing in the shade of a big tree are two round, middle-aged Mexican guys.

"*Dónde está Mexico?*" I say.

"*Aquí,*" one answers.

We introduce ourselves, reaching across the border, which is just: a monument and a stripe on the concrete.

Yellow Shirt/White Hat is Jesse. Red Shirt/Black Hat is Tomás.

"So," I say, stepping across, "this is Mexico?"

"Yes," says Tomás.

"And this is the U.S.," I say, returning to my native land.

"Yes, yes," says Jesse, stepping into the U.S. "Mexico now, now U.S."

We step giddily back and forth; straddle the line so we're in both countries simultaneously; stand on the line, declaring ourselves to be nowhere at all.

Using my arms and baby Spanish, I ask: Why don't the people, the Mexican people, come from there (I gesture to Mexico) to here (I make a grand sweep encompassing all of America and the grand opportunities contained therein).

"Problems with the *migras*," says Jesse.

"I don't see them," says Tomás. "But they see me."

We agree that Mexico and America have been good friends forever. We agree that, historically, the rich man has, forever, been stamping on—we all simultaneously perform the same gesture: stepping one foot each down on some imagined Poor Man. I snag three bottled waters from the van, and we drink to our shared respect for the worker; them in their country, me in mine. Occasionally, a foot, absentmindedly kicking at a pebble, will wander out of its own nation, or one of us will briefly emigrate to keep the sun out of his eyes.

As I pull out, a Border Patrol truck's blocking the road. The agent looks like Dwight Yoakam. Technically, he tells me, I've broken the law.

"You, uh . . . you saw me go back and forth?" I say.

"I saw you standing in Mexico," he says. "What I could do—and of course, I'm not going to DO this—is take you to Juárez and have you cross there. No biggie. But just so you know."

This, we agree, is the beauty of the United States: Here we stand, the Law and the Lawbreaker, joking about the fact that he's busted me, comfortable in the knowledge that he's not going to shake me down, as would most assuredly happen if this was, say, Juárez, where he says some drunken cops recently shot at a journalist who'd taken a photo of them getting wasted, then beat the crap out of him.

"Although how much have you got?" he says. "Ha ha!"

"How did you know I was even down there?" I say.

"Camera," he says, nodding up in the direction of the sky.

I LOVE YOU, I DO, BUT NOT IN THAT WAY

I leave Texas, drive across New Mexico, Arizona, and California, and see no sign of a crisis, no sign of an overloaded system at the point of breakdown, no crime, no discourtesy even.

Which, of course, does not mean that crises, overload, crime, and discourtesy do not exist.

It just means I didn't see them.

Everywhere I go, the next town ahead is said to be the really dangerous town, the one that justifies all the cartel fears and border paranoia, the town where the real shit goes down. Ditto for Mexicali.

I walk across the border at Calitex, and find, on the exterior wall of a strip bar, an inadvertent poem:

25 Beauty Full

Girls on Scene

Continuously dancing from 3 p.m.

Promotion.

On Buckets of Beer and Bottes

Of liquor
No cover
Charge.

But mostly, of course, Mexicali is just a town, waking up on a quiet Saturday morning: A gangly teen guy comes out of a changing room in too-baggy jeans, waits for the Judgment of Mom; a guy holds his toddler in a gentle headlock, kissing kissing kissing her repeatedly on the neck, which fails to stop her wailing; three slouching, hotted-out teenage girls loll on a bench, watching the street with eager who-might-love-me attentiveness; pigeons troop across the sunlit grass of a park like an overfed gray army. Whatever scams, corruptions, or cartel-related high jinks went down last night, all is well in the park this morning, with the bad boys still in bed.

It's a town like an American town, like the American town just across the river, in fact, if you drained half the money out and let it sit awhile. See it in fast motion: Stores close, streets go dirty, entropy increases, dark moneymaking schemes multiply, people's dreams begin to be of leaving.

This may be the one clear truth of the so-called border issue: Put a poor country next to a rich one and watch which way the traffic flows. Add impediments, the traffic endeavors to flow around them. Eliminate disparity, the traffic stops.

If Mexico were as rich as we are, we'd only be getting their tourists.

I have lunch, flirt with some local grandmothers, undercut my flirting by crotching myself on the corner of a table as I leave.

Outside, a pregnant woman displaying much cleavage, selling Chiclets on behalf of a "home for poor women," asks if I am sleeping in Mexicali tonight. It's hot and I'm tired and my mind is playing tricks and I suddenly see her as she would be if, instead of a Mexicali Chiclet-selling probable prostitute, she were a Calitex soccer mom: *The school does not properly emphasize reading; their vacation plans are proving difficult; she really hopes her daughter will stick with the cello.*

But she's not a soccer mom, she's a Mexicali Chiclet-selling probable prostitute, and in spite of the far-along state of her pregnancy, asks, several more times, with increasing urgency, where I'll be sleeping tonight, and only finally believes me when I say: America, for sure, honestly.

THOUGHT EXPERIMENT

Imagine the following scenario: Two babies are born at precisely the same moment. Baby One is healthy, with a great IQ and all its limbs and two kind, intelligent, nondysfunctional parents. Baby Two is sickly, not very bright, is missing a limb or two, and is the child of two self-absorbed and stupid losers, one of whom has not been seen around lately, the other of whom is a heroin addict.

Now imagine this scenario enacted a million times.

Now imagine those two million babies leaving the hospital and beginning to live their lives.

Statistically, the Baby Ones are going to have a better time of it than the Baby Twos. Whatever random bad luck befalls the Babies, the Baby Ones will have more resources with which to engineer a rebound. If a particular Baby One turns out to be, say, schizophrenic, he or she will get better treatment than the corresponding Baby Two, will be generally safer and better-cared-for, will more likely have a stable home to return to. Having all his limbs, he can go where he needs to go faster and easier. Ditto if Baby One is depressed, or slow-witted, or wants to be an artist, or dreams of having a family and supporting that family with dignity.

A fortunate birth, in other words, is a shock absorber.

Now we might ask ourselves: What did Baby One *do* to deserve this fortunate birth? Or, conversely, what did Baby Two *do* to deserve the unfortunate birth? Imagine the instant before birth. Even then, the die was cast. Baby Two has done nothing, exerted no will, and yet the missing limb is already missing, the slow brain already slow, the undesirable parents already undesirable. Now think back four months before birth. Is the baby any more culpable? Six months before birth? At the moment of conception? Is it possible to locate the moment when Baby Two's "culpability" begins?

Now consider a baby born with the particular neurologic condition that will eventually cause him to manifest that suite of behaviors we call "paranoia." His life will be hell. Suspicious of everyone and everything, deeply anxious, he will have little pleasure, be able to forge no deep relationships. Now here is that baby fifteen seconds after conception. All the seeds of his future condition are present (otherwise, from what would it develop?). Is he "to blame"? What did he do, what choices did he make, that caused this condition in himself? Clearly, he "did" nothing to "deserve" his paranoia. If thirty years later, suspecting that his neighbor is spying on him, he trashes the neighbor's apartment and kills the neighbor's cat with a phone book, is he "to blame"? If so, at what point in his long life was he supposed to magically overcome/transcend his condition, and how?

Here, on the other hand, is a baby born with the particular neurologic condition that will eventually cause him to manifest that suite of behaviors we call "being incredibly happy." His life will be heaven. Everything he touches will turn to gold. What doesn't turn to gold he will use as fodder for contemplation, and will be the better for it. He will be able to love and trust people and get true pleasure from them. He is capable and self-assured, and using his abilities, acquires a huge fortune and performs a long list of truly good deeds. Now here is that baby fifteen seconds after conception. All the seeds of his condition are present (otherwise, from what would it develop?). Can he, justifiably (at fifteen seconds old), "take credit for" himself? What did he do, what choices did he make, that caused this condition of future happiness to manifest? Where was the moment of the exertion of will? Where was the decision? There was no exertion of will and no decision. There was only fulfillment of a pattern that began long before his conception. So if, thirty years later, in the company of his beautiful wife, whom he loves deeply, Baby One accepts the Nobel Prize, then drives away in his Porsche, listening to Mozart, toward his gorgeous home, where his beloved children wait, thinking loving thoughts of him, can he justifiably "take credit" for any of this?

You would not blame a banana for being the banana that it is. You would not expect it to have autocorrected its bent stem or willed itself into a brighter shade of yellow. Why is it, then, so natural for us to blame a person for being the person she is, to expect her to autocorrect her shrillness, say, or to will herself into a perkier, more efficient person?

I now hear a voice from the gallery, crying: "But I am not a banana! I have made myself what I am! What about tenacity and self-improvement and persisting in our efforts until our noble cause is won?" But it seems to me that not only is our innate level of pluck, say, hardwired at birth, but also our ability to improve our level of pluck, as well as our ability to improve our ability to improve our level of pluck. All of these are ceded to us at the moment that sperm meets egg. Our life, inflected by the particulars of our experience, scrolls out from there. Otherwise, what is it, exactly, that causes Person A, at age forty, to be plucky and Person B, also forty, to be decidedly nonplucky? Is it some failure of intention? And at what point, precisely, did that failure occur?

The upshot of all of this is not a passive moral relativism that makes the bearer incapable of action in the world. If you repeatedly come to my house and drive your truck over my chickens, I had better get you arrested or have your truck taken away or somehow ironclad or elevate my chickens. But I'd contend that my ability to protect my chickens actually *improves* as I realize that your desire to flatten my chickens is organic and comes out of somewhere and is not unmotivated or even objectively evil—it is as undeniable to who you are, at that instant, as is your hair color. Which is not to say that it cannot be changed. It can be changed. It must be changed. But dropping the idea that your actions are Evil, and that you are Monstrous, I enter a new moral space, in which the emphasis is on seeing with clarity, rather than judging; on acting in the most effective way (that is, the way that most radically and permanently protects my chickens), rather than on constructing and punishing a Monster.

If, at the moment when someone cuts us off in traffic or breaks our heart or begins bombing our ancestral village, we could withdraw from judging mode, and enter this other, more accepting mode, we would, paradoxically, make ourselves more powerful. By resisting the urge to reduce, in order to subsequently destroy, we keep alive—if only for a few seconds more—the possibility of transformation.

THE
PERFECT
GERBIL

READING BARTHELME'S "THE SCHOOL"

RISE, BABY, RISE!

Sometimes, at moments of desperation in a creative writing class, I find it useful to introduce Freitag's Triangle:

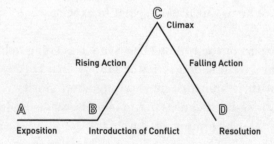

It's especially useful because I get to point to the portion labeled "Rising Action" and explain that this—*this*—is the hardest thing in storytelling: getting one's action to rise.

Sometimes at this point there are snickers in the classroom.

Whatever.

If you wanted a perfect, Platonic example of Action (Rising), you'd be hard-pressed to find a better one than Donald Barthelme's story "The School." That's essentially all it is: boldly rising action. He sets up a pattern (things associated with our school die), then escalates it. Some orange trees die, some snakes pass away, an herb garden kicks the bucket, some gerbils/mice/salamander, having been acquired by the school, cease to exist.

And we're only at paragraph three.

"The School" belongs roughly in a lineage of "pattern stories," which might be said to include, for example, Chekhov's "The Darling" (woman with no real personality of her own takes on the personalities of a series of men with whom she gets involved); Gogol's "Dead Souls" (guy goes around to a series of people, trying to buy the deeds to their dead serfs); "A Christmas Carol" (stingy man is visited by series of ghosts who try to convert him); and the stateroom scene in "Night at the Opera" (tiny room gets filled with series of people). In each of these we know, fairly early, what to expect: we grasp the pattern.

So: part of the fun of "The School" is going to be the gradual unveiling of a series of Things That Die.

But then immediately—writing short stories is very hard work—Barthelme is in trouble. The reader is already, here at the beginning of paragraph four, subtly ready to be bored. The reader knows The Pattern—and is suddenly wary that The Pattern may turn out to be all there is.

If I say: "I ate a small candy, then a bigger candy, then a candy the size of a room, then a candy the size of Montana . . . ," you get the idea. You know where I'm headed. There's a certain pleasure in this: you're in on the joke, your mind knows the general shape of the fun to be expected. But if I just keep going ("I ate a candy the size of the United States! The size of North America! The size of—" even typing this is getting tiresome, although I would have liked to get at least as far as "I ate a piece of candy the size of Uranus!"), you are going to start to dislike me. Why? Because I'm condescending. I'm assuming that this simple, linear pattern is enough to interest you. I'm treating you like a dumb beast, endlessly fascinated by a swinging weight on a cord.

A STORY IS MADE OF THINGS THAT FLING OUR LITTLE CAR FORWARD

When I was a kid I had one of these Hot Wheels devices designed to look like a little gas station. Inside the gas station were two spinning rubber wheels. One's little car would weakly approach the gas station, then be sent forth by the spinning rubber wheels to take another lap around the track or, more often, fly out and hit one's sister in the face.

A story can be thought of as a series of these little gas stations. The main point is to get the reader around the track; that is, to the end of the story. Any other pleasures a story may offer (theme, character, moral uplift) are dependent upon this.

In this case, once we've discerned the pattern, Barthelme is going to fling us forward via a series of surprises; each new pattern-element is going to be introduced in a way we don't expect, or with an embellishment that delights us. For example: when it is time for the tropical fish to be introduced, i.e., to die, Barthelme capitalizes on our knowledge (born of many carnival-won fish) that killing a tropical fish is basically a fait accompli once you've acquired one ("Those numbers, you look at them crooked and they're belly-up on the surface."). This constitutes a gas station because, in the process of advancing the pattern, he has given us a little something extra: a laugh, yes, but more important, an acknowledgment that the writer is right there with us—he knows where we are, and who we are, and is involved in an intimate and respectful game with us. I think of this as the motorcycle-sidecar model of reading: writer and reader right next to one another, leaning as they corner, the pleasure coming from the mutuality and simultaneity of the experience.

Likewise, there is a little gas station at the beginning of paragraph seven, when suddenly, from Dead Puppy, we leap to Dead Korean Orphan. This gas station has to do with the boldness of the escalation: Barthelme's refusal to flinch at the logic of his own pattern. Some part of art, certainly of Barthelme's art, involves the simple pleasure of watching someone be audacious. Another little audacity-related gas station—actually a series of gas stations, seeded throughout the story—is the pleasure we get from the narrator's stuttering, fragmented syntax, a pleasure which comes in part from our awareness that this syntax is not exactly *necessary*; it is, yes, character-indicating, but mostly it's funny, and also impressive: we take pleasure in how well it's done. Another hidden pleasure of the story is the way that the pattern is not—if I could say it this way—*load-bearing*. A lesser writer, who believes writing is about knowing, control, and mastery, told to create a pattern in which things die, might (mis)understand his job to be: designing and executing an extremely meaningful pattern. He would spend a lot of time trying to decide, in advance, the answers to questions like, "In what order should I have the things die?" and "What will I have cause the deaths?" and "How is the main character to be implicated in, and changed by, these events?"

Mr. Lesser Writer, in other words, realizing with joy that he has a pattern to work with, sits down to do some Thinking. Barthelme proceeds in a more spontaneous, vaudevillian manner. He knows that the pattern is just an excuse for the real work of the story, which is to give the reader a series of pleasure-bursts. The story, then, can be seen as a series of repetitions of one event: the reader leaves a little gas station at high speed, looking forward to the next one.

ENDING IS STOPPING
WITHOUT SUCKING

So: if the writer can put together enough gas stations, of sufficient power, distributed at just the right places around the track, he wins: the reader works his way through the full execution of the pattern, and is ready to receive the ending of the story.

Because all along, a question has been rising: OK, we've been feeling, this is funny, this is enjoyable, but how and when is it going to start being literature? How's he going to take this Marx Brothers–quality romp and convert it at the last minute into a Post-Modernist Masterpiece?

How, in other words, is this story going to *mean*?

The land of the short story is a brutal land, a land very similar, in its strictness, to the land of the joke. When I tell a joke, everyone hearing knows that the joke is going to culminate in a punch line, and the intention of the punch line is to make them laugh. If it doesn't, the joke is dumb, and I'm a dork. Likewise, when a person presumes to tell a literary short story, everyone reading knows that it is going to culminate in an ending, and that the intention of the ending is to . . .

Well, hold on—what *is* the intention of the ending?

Or—the million-dollar question for any of us who has ever tried to complete a short story: When constitutes a *sufficient* ending? In other words, what does Barthelme have to do here, as he goes forth from the end of paragraph nine (which I consider the end of the Rising Action), so that we will continue to love him?

His first responsibility is to not do something that will make us groan. What will make us groan? Something that too neatly "answers to" his Pattern.

Say he ended it:

Then I came in one day, and all the kids were dead.
And all of a sudden I wasn't feeling so good myself!
That was one bad semester!
THE END!

This is not a story ending, but the ending of a lousy after-dinner speech; it knows its own pattern too well, and has stuck with it mindlessly, to the bitter end. It has done (merely) what it set out to do—and we require more of our endings than this.

Einstein once said something along the lines of: "No worthy problem is ever solved within the plane of its original conception." Touching on the same idea, a famous poet once said: "If you set out to write a poem about two dogs fucking, and you write a poem about two dogs fucking, then you've written a poem about two dogs fucking."

What we want our ending to do is to do more than we could have dreamed it would do.

Sheesh.

No wonder there's such a thing as writer's block.

But Barthelme understands that what he has to do in this last page is keep doing what has worked so far in the story: he has to escalate. The story has, so far, been captivating us via its nervy continual progress along the axis labeled: Deaths, Increasing. By paragraph nine (parents have died, fellow students have died) Barthelme's gone about as far along that axis as he can, and now understands that, to continue escalating, he has to leap to another axis. He seems to intuit that the next order of escalation has to be *escalating* escalation.

"One day," he tells us, "we had a discussion in class. They asked me, where did they go? The trees, the salamander, the tropical fish, Edgar, the poppas and mommas, Matthew and Tony, where did they go? And I said, I don't know, I don't know. And they said, who knows? and I said, nobody knows."

So there's a possible ending, right? He's turned to look back at his pattern, he's addressed it—he's wryly yet earnestly commented on it, saying a true thing: nobody knows why death happens. It's not bad. But it's not great. One can almost feel Barthelme squirming under the not-greatness of it, then pushing discontentedly onward, feeling around with his most substantial tool: the devastating adroitness of his language. Our narrator continues: "And they said, is death that which gives meaning to life?" (We notice this weird, illogical elevation of diction—three lines ago these kids were still saying "poppas and mommas.") "And I said, no, life is that which gives meaning to life." (We like that the narrator doesn't balk at his students' sudden new articulateness—he doesn't even acknowledge it—maybe, it occurs to us, they talk like this all the time?) "Then they said, but isn't death, considered as a fundamental datum, the means by which the taken-for-granted—"

Whoa, we think, slow down, they're now talking in an even *more* elevated—

". . . mundanity of the everyday may be transcended in the direction of—"

What's happening here, I think, is that Barthelme's mind has gotten tired of being polite. Without worrying about whether it's allowed, or will be understood, or is logical within the world of the story (or whether the workshop will tolerate it), he races off in the direction his logic is taking him, appropriate diction be damned, trying to get the story to answer the questions the thing's been asking all along: What are we to make of death? How are we to live in a world where death is king?

We follow because we find his courage thrilling.

Does he then use this new allowance we've granted him—this expanded diction—to glibly wrap the story up on some cool philosophical basis? ("Then little Sally Adams posited that, what manifested to them as mundanity could also be understood as simply as an example of Brugenheiser's 'vantage conundrum,' at which time the bell rang, and they bolted from their desks, well-satisfied with Sally's explanation, and our day was done, as all our days, eventually, will be done, for all of us, for good.")

No, thank God, he does not.

He escalates again. The students (still in professorial diction) request that he make love with Helen. Where does this come from? Until just now, there was no Helen. Sorry, Don's in a hurry, and can't/won't explain it to us, except to let us know, parenthetically, that Helen is "our teaching assistant." "Come on, come on!" he seems to be saying. "It surprised me too! Just keep up!"

Will they do it? Will the narrator and Helen make love? The reader honestly doesn't know, but does care. The narrator demurs: "I said I would be fired and that it was never, or almost never, done as a demonstration." (The "or almost never" is a fine little gas station.)

And then the reader (this reader, anyway) falls, once and for all, forever, in love with this story, at the line: "Helen looked out of the window." Why? Well, for one thing, Helen *wants* to do it, and *will* do it, in front of the class, gladly, if only The Narrator will ask. She has loved him all along. A few lines ago we didn't even know Helen existed, but we do now, and so does The Narrator, and the small voice in our mind that has all along been registering that The Narrator has no personal life in this story, that there are no real human emotions in the story, that this alleged story is just a pattern, is assuaged: this is now, writ small, a love story. It's a love story! We see Helen plainly, her sensible shoes, the red-ink stains on her young hands, which she wrings every evening in her tiny, under-furnished, teacher's assistant apartment, dreaming of a life with The Narrrator. But Helen is shy! She doesn't want to demand anything! She's not a pushy girl, our Helen—

But also—there is no Helen. Or, there's barely a Helen. Helen has only existed for four short paragraphs, and already she represents quiet, faithful, unrequited love. Our pleasure in Helen is, partly, also pleasure in Barthelme's incredible economy.

Little four-paragraph Helen sits, drumming her ink-stained fingers, gazing out the window, waiting, hoping . . .

The children press their case, and we see that making love with Helen would be a real win/win/win; not only would Helen like it, The Narrator seems kind of lonely, and it would also be good, you know, for the kids ("We require an assertion of value," they plead, "we are frightened.").

Weirdly, we are really curious, or at least I always am, to see if some lovemaking will in fact break out on this desk somewhere in the desolate, death-besieged Midwest, or what.

We have one long paragraph left.

And look what's happened: suddenly, Barthelme can end this thing any way he pleases. The essential work has been done. If the narrator begins making love to Helen, that's good. If he declines, also good. The air is charged with meaning. It is everywhere we look. It seems he's going to pass—he kisses Helen on the brow—but we sense that he and Helen may very soon be demonstrating some lovemaking, if only to one another, possibly in Helen's sparse apartment. Everything has changed between them. Suddenly there is death in the room, but also life, and love.

The reader is satisfied: so much has happened, in so short a time and in such an unexpected way. It could end with a simple line: "I looked at Helen, and she looked at me."

But Barthelme, being great, abides long enough to produce from his sleeve one last escalation which, Barthelme being Barthelme, arrives in the person (?) of a gerbil.

Where does the gerbil come from? How did it find the classroom? And why is it a gerbil and not (if we are seeking circularity) an orange tree, or at least a snake? How did it knock on the door? Doesn't it know this is exactly the wrong class, that soon it will die? Or—who can say?—maybe Helen's just-revealed love for The

Narrator's love has changed everything, and the gerbil will live, and prosper, and get fat enough to overflow its cage!

It is ambiguous, and it is funny, and somehow perfect: this little expectant rodent, politely waiting for its knock to be answered, all set to die, or to live.

We, like the children, "cheer wildly."

THE
UNITED STATES
OF HUCK

INTRODUCTION TO *ADVENTURES OF HUCKLEBERRY FINN*

INTRODUCTION TO THE
INTRODUCTION

Let me begin by confessing that I have had more trouble with this piece than I've ever had writing anything in my life, mainly because I love this book and was deathly afraid I would fail to do it justice, which caused me to rush off to the library and do hours and hours of research, which only terrified me further and reduced me to writing quaking tautological sentences like "Much has been written about the fact that much has been written about the fact that, whereas the shores of the Mississippi, mythologically speaking, represent America's violence, the center of the river, which traditionally has been represented as Utopian, is also occasionally seen to contain bloated floating corpses." Recognizing that my sentences were perhaps not as clear as they could be, I began furiously editing, bearing in mind at every instant that *Adventures of Huckleberry Finn* is probably the greatest and certainly the most influential American novel of all time, and has inspired feelings of fierce love and loyalty in every important American writer, except in those other important American writers who have really, really disliked it and found it morally problematic, and soon I had worked myself into such a state of bowing obeisance and timidity that my sentences became a bland series of tenuous apologetic nouns, no verbs at all, as these, I felt, were too risky.

But luckily that phase is past, and I can now, using quite a number of verbs, espouse a Tentative Narrative Theory regarding *Huck Finn.*

A TENTATIVE NARRATIVE THEORY REGARDING *HUCK FINN*

Have you ever been in an airport and seen those escalators whose purpose it is not to actually escalate, but to move people horizontally, which is why they are called people movers? Imagine the novelist as a person standing at one end of a people mover, with a shovel, in front of a big pile of dirt. The pile of dirt represents The Thing This Writer Loves To Do, And Does Naturally. The writer started writing so that he or she could endlessly and effortlessly do this thing and nothing else— be funny, say, or verbally brilliant, or write lush nature vignettes, or detailed descriptions of the interiors of rich people's houses—and then be declared Wonderful, and buy a nicer car. But all writers soon find that their Dirt is not enough. Yes, their readership stands at the far end of the people mover, eagerly awaiting this Dirt, but if the writer simply dumps shovelful after shovelful of Dirt onto the people mover, the people mover grinds to a halt, and the readership walks away to see a movie. Three hundred pages of descriptions of rich people's houses will not cut it: the writer must connect the dots of Dirt with something else, something narrative, something that imitates forward motion. The people mover must be fed Dirt a little at a time, so that it will keep moving, and in this way, and this way only, the readership will in time receive all the Dirt the writer wishes to administer.

Now, to extend this already rickety metaphor, let us say that what keeps the people mover moving is what we will call the Apparent Narrative Rationale. The Apparent Narrative Rationale is what the writer and the reader have tacitly agreed the book is "about." In most cases, the Apparent Narrative Rationale is centered around simple curiosity: the reader understands that he is waiting to learn if Scrooge will repent, if Romeo will marry Juliet, if the crops will be saved, the widow rescued. While the reader waits for that answer, the writer gets a chance to create the Three Christmas Ghosts and compose the Balcony Speech, and in the end, the reader finds that this—the Dirt—is what he or she has wanted all along.

The Apparent Narrative Rationale, then, can be seen as the writer's answer to his own question: "What exactly is it that I am doing here?"

I now skillfully segue back to Mark Twain, aka Samuel Clemens.

Twain is the funniest literary American writer, and his funniness is so energetic and true and pure that it must have been a great pleasure to be him, sitting there dressed all in white, smoking cigar after cigar in your hexagonal study, with the pure funniness pouring out of the top of your head, helping you combat your native grouchiness. Like many lower-class writers (Chekhov, Dickens, Gogol come to mind), he started his career being purely funny, in comic sketches that were mostly Dirt and very little people mover, and all his writing life struggled with the question of what his Apparent Narrative Rationale should be, which is why he left behind such a long trail of abandoned manuscripts. He was not an outliner, not a planner, did not establish an agenda and carry it through, but wrote as the spirit moved him, in as improvisatory a manner as any writer ever did. "Mr. Clemens," wrote William Dean Howells, his friend and editor, "is the first writer to use in extended writing the fashion we all use in thinking, and to set down the thing that comes into his mind without fear or favor of the thing that went before or the thing that may be about to follow. . . . [H]e would take whatever offered itself to his hand out of that mystical chaos, that divine ragbag, which we call the mind, and leave the reader to look after relevancies and sequences for himself."

Huck Finn was written in three or four distinct bursts of creativity, between which Twain put the manuscript away and wrote plays no one has ever heard of and invented machines no one has ever used. Each time he stopped, he apparently did so for the simplest of reasons: he didn't know how to keep going. He lost faith in his Apparent Narrative Rationale, or interest in it, or found that it had led him to some seemingly insoluble narrative problem, and so put the book aside and invented an Invisible Ink Typewriter or a Systematic Noodle Identifier. Each time he came back to the book, he did so with renewed enthusiasm and a new plan on how to proceed: a new Apparent Narrative Rationale. This sequence of Apparent Narrative Rationales may be roughly described as follows: (1) I Will Rewrite *Tom Sawyer*, but from Huck's Point of View; (2) I Will Take Huck and Jim Up the River, Ostensibly to Freedom; (3) I Will Write a Treatise on the Mores and Manners of the American Southwest; (4) I Will Build This Whole Deal Up into One of the Most Beautiful Moments of Impending Action Ever, in Which We See That Huck Must Risk His Life to Single-handedly Save Jim; and (5) I Will Let Tom Sawyer Come Inexplicably Back into My Story and Ruin My Ending.

Now, all fiction writers labor under this burden of not-knowing. "The writer," said Donald Barthelme, "is one who, embarking upon a task, does not know what to do." In this mode of not-knowing, the thick-torsoed, literal, and crew-cut conscious mind is moved to the sidelines in favor of the swinging, perceptive, light-footed, tutu-wearing subconscious. We surprise ourselves, and make something bigger than we could have imagined making before we started trying to make it. But as Twain wrote *Huck Finn*, his not-knowing seems also to have been operating on a second and more profound level. All those adjustments of his Apparent Narrative Rationales took place in part because his book was making him uncomfortable. His comic novel was doing things a comic novel was not supposed to do, and yet he sort of liked it, and yet, come to think of it, it was really pretty darn uncomfortable, and he didn't yet feel like fighting the battles his story was presaging. In effect, his subconscious was urging him to do things his conscious mind didn't know could be done, or didn't particularly want done, and so my Tentative Narrative Theory is simply this: the tension between various warring parts of Sam Clemens—the radical and the reactionary; the savage satirist and the kindly Humorist; the raw hick and the aspiring genteel Literary Figure—is what makes *Huck Finn* such a rich and formidable book.

That is all the narrative theory I have at the moment, but I will return to this question of Twain's understanding of his own book later, after I dispense with the question of whether *Huck Finn* is indeed a Great Novel or if, on the other hand, the millions of people who have read and loved it and felt that it was morally important and gorgeous have all been stupid and deceived and hopelessly old-fashioned and dupable.

WHAT'S SO GREAT ABOUT IT?

Twain started the book in 1876, as a companion piece to one he had recently finished, *The Adventures of Tom Sawyer*, but with a critical difference: he would tell the new story from the point of view of its main character, Huck Finn, son of the town drunk. "I shall take a boy of twelve & run him through life (in the first person)," Twain wrote to Howells in 1875. This first-person voice turned out to be one of the most natural and poetic literary voices ever devised, a voice still startling in its ability to bring the physical world (predawn birdcalls, a tin drainpipe on a moonlit night, the mud-smell of a river at dawn) off the page and into our heads, making us feel as if we hadn't merely read the scenes but lived them, over and over, in some parallel and primal universe. It is this voice that first gets us, and it is this feeling of love for the voice—our delight in Huck's common sense, his original way of thinking, the perfect roll and cadence of these odd sentences, so unliterary by the standards of Twain's time—that first, I expect, put into some early critic's head the idea that the book was not just a boy's book, not just a quasi-naughty work of low comedy, but in fact, a great and seminal work of art. With this voice, Twain threw open the door on an America previously unrepresented in our literature: its lower classes, its hustlers and religious con men, possessed of equal parts Spirit and Lust; its leaning frame houses, inside of which corpulent men, tended by slaves, read aloud from Bibles. In an era when Whitman and Emerson were linking the health of the American democracy to its downward inclusiveness, along came *Huck Finn*, which was so terrifically downwardly inclusive that it was banned by the Concord Library for "dealing with a series of experiences not elevating."

The voice is what hooks so many young writers on the book, and inspires them to attempt to do for our time what Twain did for his, which is why every few years there appears some new work described as "a *Huck Finn*-like reverie on freedom and constraint, set in a convent, in which Sister Gertrude, like Huck, dreams of climbing out the window and having a smoke" or "like *Huck Finn*, if Huck Finn was raised in Cleveland and Pap was not a cruel drunk but a sort of cranky rabbi." But this tendency of *Huck Finn* to cause other writers to write books extremely similar to it but worse is telling; the voice of the book reminds us of the beauty of the world, and of the fact that that beauty can indeed be gotten at by the word, and that our language, English, that old dowager, has not yet begun to fight. As long as there is a new reality, the voice tells us, English too will be new, and it is you, the young writer, who will make it so. And so off the young writers go, trying to figure out what their River is, and who their Jim is, and what America's current most noxious trait is, so they can lampoon it. And although— at least the three or four times I've tried it—the final product is not a book at all, but a pile of papers you fling across the room; the final product is also a new respect for the originality and genius of the book, and for Twain, of whom F. Scott Fitzgerald once said, beautifully: "His eyes were the first eyes that ever looked at us objectively that were not eyes from overseas."

In *Huck Finn*, the landscape appears to us on a strangely human scale: we feel ourselves actually moving through it. I don't know if this is true for anybody else, but when I read, my inner eye is normally situated about ten feet off the ground. I look down on Dostoevsky's characters as if perched beside some icon on a beet-smelling shelf; when Bob Cratchit tests the Christmas pudding, I'm up on the stove, which fortunately for me is one of those instantaneously cooling Victorian stoves. When I read *Huck Finn*, though, I am Huck's height, looking up at all these unkempt hostile people looking down at me, grazing a tree with my arm, running a finger through the dust that has settled on an end table in that magnificently described Grangerford parlor, killing an actual pig, letting the hand that killed the pig trail behind me in the green waters of the Mississippi.

The person who tries to list all that is wonderful about *Huck Finn* will soon find that his family has fled, the grass has overgrown the sidewalk, the dog has starved to death, and his life is over. There is wonderfulness everywhere you look, and from whatever angle you look. I would guess that a person could wade into the book with any idea in mind ("Christianity," or "the forest," or "concepts of feminine beauty") and find that idea not only represented in *Huck Finn* but metaphorically developed, and metaphorically developed in a way that simultaneously sheds light on Twain, the reader, and the cosmos. Try it yourself; read it, say, with "concepts of

feminine beauty" in mind, and you will soon find yourself convinced that Twain only invented the stuff about
the kid and the slave and the big river and freedom and
democracy as a diversionary tactic so he could really sink
his teeth into the concept of feminine beauty.

Such metaphorical suppleness comes, I think, in proportion to how purely the artistic product proceeds from
the subconscious, and from the quality of that subconscious. Twain's subconscious was a formidable thing—
he had been just about everywhere in America, usually
at a time when something big was happening, had done
that most purely American thing, namely work himself
above his original station, had begun his life as a lower-
middle-class kid in a slave-owning household, which situated him squarely on the twin issues that make every
American sweat and frown and burst into defensiveness
and begin spouting groundless platitudes, namely race
and class—and when this subconscious took charge,
emboldened by a temporarily perplexed conscious mind,
the book wrote itself out of any known genre and into
this wild new thing we are still trying to classify and
make sense of.

So there is the voice, and the created world along the
river, and the amazing assortment of characters, and
the constantly shifting skein of metaphors, and the rich
stinging humor—but what truly animates the book, and
makes it so dangerous and transcendent and even pre-
scient, is the relationship between Huck and Jim.

THE CENTRAL MORAL VECTOR

Huck is an ignorant white-trash boy. Not only is he
white trash, he is the lowest of the white trash, sort

of White-Trash Trash, because his father is the town drunk. And this town drunk is not of the Amiable Nostalgic school of town-drunkery but of the Brutal Violent school. Huck flees town, to escape Pap and the equally oppressive if less flamboyant Righteous Spinster Duo, Miss Watson and the Widow Douglas, and soon is faced with a dilemma: this dilemma is named Jim, and Jim is an escaped slave, and all of Huck's training thus far has been that slavery is good, biblically sanctioned even, and that he should always do what is right, which in this case means he should turn Jim in. Bearing in mind our human fondness for establishing ourselves as Worthwhile by kicking someone beneath us simply because we can, especially if we ourselves have been repeatedly kicked, it would not be surprising if Huck, who has no mother and no real home and a father who locks him in a shed and beats him, were to take a little pleasure from mistreating Jim. (Imagine a sort of contemporary Huck-equivalent: a little community-despised white-trash boy, son of an American Nazi Party member who periodically beats him and locks him in the garage for days, comes upon a sleeping and vulnerable homeless black man—what might he do?) And yet all of Huck's instincts tell him that Jim is a man, and a friend, and we come to see that Jim cares about Huck more genuinely, with more real affection, than anyone else in the book, and so the Central Moral Vector lies in the question: Will Huck turn Jim in?

Huck struggles with this question, and watching this struggle we come to love him, and conducting this struggle, he becomes one of the great figures of world literature. "No one who reads thoughtfully the dialectic of Huck's moral crisis," Lionel Trilling said, "will ever again be wholly able to accept without some question and some irony the assumptions of the respectable morality by which he lives."

Anyway, this is what we are told, and taught, and what we remember about the book years later: the book is about the question of whether Huck, this probable nascent racist, will transcend himself and help Jim realize his dream of freedom. This question hangs over the entire book and, to the contemporary mind, gives it the shape that allows us to argue for its noble moral intent, and to assess its artistic triumph or failure, but the truth is, there are entire sections of the book that behave as if this question had not been asked. Jim spends a good deal of the middle portion of the book effectively neutralized as a narrative player, hidden on board the raft or in the woods, with his face painted blue and/or tied hand and foot and/or dressed up like King Lear. There are other places where Jim fades into caricature, and in these places it seems as if Twain—involved in the writing of the book and not in its analysis many years later, flailing around in search of his Apparent Narrative Rationale, still emerging from the slog of his childhood racial attitudes, trying on different models of what his book was, inventing and reinventing his Upside-Down Lapel Reinstator—has forgotten what his book is about, or at least has forgotten what, many years later, we will claim his book is about.

All of what is debated and sometimes deplored about *Huck Finn*—its structural problems, its weak ending, its racism—can, I contend, be traced back to the fact that Twain only dimly and imperfectly understood that his book had a Central Moral Vector. Or rather, he knew, but sometimes forgot. Or rather, he knew, but periodically got interested in other aspects of the book and lost sight of it. Or maybe, and most interestingly: his Central Moral Vector was too hot to handle, and would have required him to simultaneously invent, understand, and complete his book in an entirely new genre, a genre that neither Twain nor the world was quite ready for.

THE ENDING, OH MY GOD,
THE ENDING

Twain's failure to love, honor, and obey his Central Moral Vector is most gut-droppingly apparent in the ending. "In the whole reach of the English novel, there is not a more abrupt or chilling descent," wrote Bernard DeVoto, one of our great Twain scholars, and since we are heaping scorn on the ending, I may as well quote Leo Marx, another one of our great Twain scholars, who said that the ending "jeopardizes the significance of the entire novel." Even Hemingway, who loved the book, and whose famous quote about it ("All modern American literature comes from one book by Mark Twain called *Huckleberry Finn*. It's the best book we've had. . . . There was nothing before . . .") is required for any introduction (and so I have now discharged that duty, with apologies to Melville and Poe and Hawthorne, who might feel that their books had at least a little something to do with modern American literature)—even Hemingway suggested that the reader stop reading before the end of the book, which, since Hemingway is no longer with us and therefore cannot beat me up, I have to say strikes me as a bit of a cop-out: the book has an ending, and Twain loved that ending, and wrote it in what was basically a transport of ecstasy in the summer of 1876, sometimes working from breakfast to dinner, and never disclaimed it afterward but proudly and successfully read from it on the book's reading tour.

Having said all this, I will also say that there is a kind of perverse greatness in the ending, in the sense that Waterloo was a great last battle for someone as considerable as Napoleon. Some part of Twain realized what he had brought himself to the brink of, and great talent that he was, he did not tarry on the brink of that cliff, or pretend there was no cliff, or that he was not standing at the edge of it: instead he ran at high speed back the way he'd come, causing a disaster, but one that is on as grand a scale as the novel itself.

SO WHAT'S WRONG WITH IT, EXACTLY?

For me, the most moving part of the book is the scene at the end of chapter 23. Jim tells Huck about the time he slapped his young daughter in the head for not obeying him, only to find that she had never actually heard him: she had gone deaf from a recent bout with scarlet fever. It's a heartbreaker, as I was reminded just now when I went to get the chapter reference, reread it, and started bawling. Any parent reading this is sickened with the magnitude and hurtfulness of Jim's error, with the impossibility of ever really erasing it, and—this is a particular manifestation of Twain's moral genius—with the fact that, horrible as this mistake would have been for any parent, this parent is a slave, a thousand miles from a home he will probably never get back to, if the prevailing national culture has its way.

We leave this scene with our sense of the Central Moral Vector confirmed: Huck's dawning realization of Jim's humanity is essential to the story, and Twain knows it.

Eighty pages or so later, Huck finds out that Jim has been sold and is being imprisoned, and has to decide what to do. There follows one of the most famous and wonderful passages in any literature, in which Huck decides, finally, to purposely do what he knows to be wrong—free Jim—and thus doom himself to hell. It is a brilliant hymn to clear-sightedness and against hypocrisy, and when you read it with the memory of the above-mentioned scene still fresh in your mind, the effect is to be slingshotted toward what now feels like the inevitable ending: Huck, who has lied and tricked his way down the river, will now lie and trick Jim free, or will try to.

Twain has written himself into a tough and very serious spot. Jim is being held prisoner in the Deep South by people used to holding prisoners, people who do not have wishy-washy opinions about slaves, or what to do with them, or what to do with people, even little boys, who help them escape. Three ideas, which Twain has skillfully nurtured throughout the book, come together: (1) Huck has transcended himself; (2) Jim is the best and most genuine human being in the book; and (3) the violence that has been intensifying and coming closer to Jim and Huck throughout the novel is now nearly upon them. And suddenly we feel, as perhaps Twain did, that the book has written itself out of its rollicking comic tradition and into something else, something more tragic and frightening, that would indict America in a way America would not soon forget.

Because what should happen is something deeply sad. Jim cannot escape, not for long, and Huck cannot remain unpunished for having helped Jim escape: the country Twain has made is too cruel and sure of itself and methodical in its slavery for either of these things to happen. And Twain understood the book—as we do—to be a comic novel, and the prospect of Jim being sold down the river or lynched, and Huck being bullwhipped and/or sent to a reformatory, say, does not gibe with our expectations of a comic novel, where violence happens only to side players, and generally off-camera, and usually because they deserve it.

So what does Twain do? This literary purist, who had lambasted James Fenimore Cooper for his too-lengthy canoes and exaggeratedly hearing-gifted Indians, commits one of the worst Coincidences in the history of writing. Huck approaches the house where Jim is being held, planning to enact another swindle, and a woman comes out, mistakes him for another little boy (we flinch a bit at this; mistaken identity has been used maybe once too often in the book), and then—horror of horrors—we learn that this other little boy's name is Tom, and we begin whispering to ourselves, *No way, no way, Mark, Sam, don't do it*—but our worst fears are soon confirmed: this woman is Tom Sawyer's aunt, and she—here, eleven hundred miles upriver—is expecting a visit from Tom himself *any minute now.*

Now, a coincidence is all right, life is full of them, but a reader's willingness to ingest one is inversely related to how badly the writer needs one, and Twain needed one very badly at this point, to avoid stepping into the dangerous trap his subconscious had set for him.

So at the moment when Huck seems most complete, heroic, and alive, Tom Sawyer, that Europhile, that conceptualizer, that American Philistine, comes flying up the river to save Twain from his own book.

A WORD ABOUT TOM,
THAT STINKER

Tom Sawyer is likable enough in *The Adventures of Tom Sawyer*, tolerable in the opening chapters of *Huck Finn*, where he serves mostly as a marker for how much more humane and sensible Huck is. In those early chapters, Huck grows increasingly skeptical of Tom's imitative and book-toadying and derivative style of adventure, and seemingly leaves him behind forever in the famous line "It had all the marks of a Sunday School." Then it's out on the river for Huck, eleven hundred miles of adventure and tricks and self-reliance and encounters with grown men, from which he emerges triumphant, saved again and again by his own common sense and wit, while presumably Tom is back home, dipping pigtails in inkwells and whining about how Sid is teasing him too much and so forth.

The difference between Tom and Huck is that Huck believes in the reality of what he sees and feels, and Tom does not. Tom believes in what he has read in books, or, more correctly, in the concepts that have arisen from what he has read in books. Huck believes in the reality of the people and things he sees, whereas, to Tom, these things are only imperfect imitations of the people and things about which he has read. Because Huck believes that other people are real, he also believes in the reality of their suffering; he grieves when he hurts Jim, worries about the drunken rider at the circus, feels bad for betraying Miss Watson, and, most importantly, understands how much Jim needs his freedom. To Tom, Jim is not real, nor is Jim's suffering; Jim's suffering is simply an opportunity for Tom's ego and cleverness to exert themselves. He prolongs and worsens this suffering by putting Jim through an insane ritual of escape à la those in Walter Scott novels (the low-comic riff that was Twain's Apparent Narrative Rationale at that time) and by withholding from Jim the staggering truth: Jim has been free for most of the novel, because Miss Watson emancipated him on her deathbed.

Tom and Huck, of course, correspond to different parts of their creator. Tom, perhaps, to that part of Twain that longed for acceptance from the Snooty East, and Superior Europe, and distrusted the Huck part—so crude, wild, backwoodsy, and unschooled. Literary characters can come only from their creator's psyche, but in this case—maybe because Twain's psyche was such a specimen psyche, and because he had such unfettered access to it—his personal binary was also a critical national one: Huck and Tom represent two viable models of the American Character. They exist side by side in every American and every American action. America is, and always has been, undecided about whether it will be the United States of Tom or the United States of Huck. The United States of Tom looks at misery and says: Hey, I didn't do it. It looks at inequity and says: All my life I have busted my butt to get where I am, so don't come crying to me. Tom likes kings, codified nobility, unquestioned privilege. Huck likes people, fair play, spreading the truck around. Whereas Tom knows, Huck wonders. Whereas Huck hopes, Tom presumes. Whereas Huck cares, Tom denies. These two parts of the American Psyche have been at war since the beginning of the nation, and come to think of it, these two parts of the World Psyche have been at war since the beginning of the world, and the hope of the nation and of the world is to embrace the Huck part and send the Tom part back up the river, where it belongs.

But this is not what happens in Huck Finn.

Instead, Huck-Growing becomes Huck-Stultified. His clarity and moral resolve fade and he becomes, if anything, more of a passive Sawyer-lackey than he was at the beginning of the book. Jim falls off the shelf of the human entirely. He allows himself to be bitten by rats, writes notes on the wall in his own blood, does not escape though there is a clear route of escape, participates in Tom's idiotic rituals without a word of objection. Convinced of the holiness of Huck's mission, we are forced to watch that mission reduced to a sickening vaudeville sketch.

"Having only half-escaped the genteel tradition, one of whose preeminent characteristics was an optimism undaunted by disheartening truth," Santayana wrote, "[Twain] returned to it."

LET'S BURN IT, THEN BAN IT, THEN BURN IT AGAIN

Even before its publication, *Huck Finn* was at the center of a controversy involving one of its illustrations, which had been changed by an ornery typographer who put a certain part of Uncle Silas's anatomy outside his pants rather than inside them, and made it look something like an angry duck. Original objections to the book itself centered around the issue of its crudeness. The book was a shocking portrayal of a white-trash boy who smoked, snuck out windows barefoot, sat around naked on a raft, smoked some more, told a bunch of lies, then openly expressed a desire to go to hell. Over the years, as the much-feared epidemic of young boys sneaking out of windows barefoot while smoking and wishing to go to hell never materialized, the crudity objection faded, replaced by another: the book and its author were racist. Or maybe just the book was racist. Or maybe the author was partly racist, which infected the book, which basically had its heart in the right place.

In "Mark Twain and His Times," Arthur G. Pettit paints a picture of Twain as a man who started out life a natural, enculturated racist and gradually grew out of it, or as out of it as his time and culture permitted. Twain was the son of a slave owner, in a town of slave owners. As a boy he saw his father administer beatings and floggings and once saw a fellow townsman crush a slave's head with an iron bar. Near the real-life model for *Huck Finn*'s Jackson Island, young Clemens found the disemboweled body of a murdered slave, and at fourteen he witnessed the lynching of a black man accused of raping a white woman. Before and during the time of the Civil War, according to Pettit, Twain "ranted against 'niggers' and told a long series of popular jokes about 'nigger odor,' fried 'nigger' steaks, black sexual promiscuity, and the evils of miscegenation." But by the 1880s Twain had changed; he made impassioned speeches against race brutality, paid the Yale tuition of several black students, became friends with Frederick Douglass and Booker T. Washington. In short, his natural clearheadedness asserted itself on the issue of racial equality, and it was out of this spirit that *Huck Finn* came.

But given Twain's roots, it would be surprising if the book's representation of blacks didn't bear some evidence of its author's journey. And it does. There are moments, even before the ending, when the "real" Jim—that is,

the Jim we perceive through, or in spite of, Huck's fore-
shortened first-person presentation of him—is not fully
human but a minstrelish caricature, moments when we
sense that somewhere in the back of Twain's mind, some
swaggering remnant of the Hannibal kid is cranking out
stereotypical comic images of blacks for cheap laughs,
images that Twain the Reformed is failing to fully reject.
It is wholly appropriate that Jim be a believable slave,
subject to all the restrictions, educational and otherwise,
that that word implies, but there is no need for him to be
an idiot. And there are places in the book where Jim is
presented as simpleminded, almost retarded, and these
places are in stark contrast to other places where we see
him as an intelligent, kind, wary, adult runaway, doing
his best to balance his natural goodness against his fear
of recapture, his justifiable suspicion of Huck against his
real affection for the boy.

The questions about race in *Huck Finn* tend to center around the presence in the book of the word "nigger,"
but my guess is that, if the book were free of the types of
missteps described above, and if the ending weren't such
a fiasco, that word might not be such a problem. That is,
if our wishful dream of the book (in which Jim is always
fully human and three-dimensional, and in which Huck
steadily and then definitively comes to understand this)
had been perfectly realized, I think most readers would
tolerate the *n*-word as an important and even essential
indicator of character. It is crucial that we understand
Huck as a possible nascent racist, and so he had better
talk like one. Imagine a story about the possible salvation
of a young misogynist, son of a radical woman-hater;
the story is nonsense if that budding misogynist and
his creepy father speak of women only in the purest and
most enlightened terms.

Having said that, I will also say that a writer who uses the *n*-word (which even in Twain's day was understood to be derogatory) walks a fine moral line. He or she can do one of three things with the *n*-word (or other ethnic slurs, or gender pejoratives): (1) use it less than it would "actually" be used, that is, omit or decrease its use by people who might reasonably be expected, by virtue of their class or education or stupidity, to use it; (2) use it exactly as much as it "should" be used, that is, use it whenever it seems that a given character would indeed use it, and when its use is thematically essential; or (3) use it *more* than it would actually be used, that is, use it gratuitously, swaggeringly. Which was Twain doing? Was Twain swaggering? Do we detect any swaggering? If so, is this possible apparent swaggering only an accurate imitation of the actual ambient swaggering of his boyhood Hannibal? At this point in the argument, one starts to get a nauseated, bean-countery feeling: Can we ever really know to what extent this man or his book was, or is, racist? When we identify racism in the book, aren't we really just identifying racism in the culture out of which it came? Is it fair to expect Twain to have vaulted himself out of his own time and place and arrive, clean-booted and upright, in our own? Isn't the book still funny and deep? Aren't I actually enjoying it? How does one do the complicated math of Ultimate Racism: If we determine that, relative to our time, Twain was a 40 percent racist, while relative to his own, he was only a 12 percent racist, or was in fact a 0 percent racist—what do we know, really?

And yet the question of race in *Huck Finn* matters very much, if you are the young black man or woman who, reading the book, is made uncomfortable or ashamed by it, or if, conversely, you are the young white man or woman who, reading the book, has some secret feelings of race superiority inflamed. It matters a lot, and it is very complicated. That the book is beautiful and thrilling is undeniable. That parts of it make the contemporary reader queasy is also undeniable. That the book and its author had an antiracist intent is also undeniable. That the author did not fulfill that intent as purely as he would have, had he been born in our time rather than his own, but with the exact same talent, having had exactly the same life experiences, is also undeniable, as well as completely nonsensical. We got Twain when we got him, and thank goodness we did, and God help the culture that pretends that earlier stupidities never happened and tries to eradicate all evidence of them.

Maybe the best we can do is concede that the book is beautiful and difficult, and that its beauties and its difficulties are inseparably linked, and then try to understand (and teach) that the book's racial problems can be dissected and understood narratively—that is, in terms of how stories are told and received—and that we are all empowered by the process of undertaking this sort of investigation. The problems with race in *Huck Finn* can best be understood as narrative problems, technical problems, and the process of discerning and understanding these technical problems is a noble process, and the ability to discern and understand these problems is an essential ability. In a culture that is becoming ever more story-stupid, in which a representative of the Coca-Cola company can, with a straight face, pronounce, as he donates a collection of archival Coca-Cola commercials to the Library of Congress, that "Coca-Cola has become an integral part of people's lives by helping to tell these stories," it is perhaps not surprising that people have trouble teaching and receiving a novel as complex and flawed as *Huck Finn*, but it is even more urgent that we learn to look passionately and technically at stories, if only to protect ourselves from the false and manipulative ones being circulated among us.

AT LAST I'M DONE, AND YOU CAN GO READ IT

Art, at its best, is a kind of uncontrolled yet disciplined Yelp, made by one of us who, because of the brain he was born with and the experiences he has had and the training he has received, is able to emit a Yelp that contains all of the joys, miseries, and contradictions of life as it is actually lived. That Yelp, which is not a logical sound, does good for all of us. Chekhov said that the purpose of art is not to solve problems but to formulate them correctly, and in *Huck Finn*, Twain formulated our national problems in a joyful and madly funny and frightening Yelp that amounted to a national clearing of the throat. It is kind of insane, this book, but in the same way that tribal cultures immunize and strengthen themselves by sitting around watching some half-nutty shaman flail around spouting descriptions of his mad vision, we are improved by Twain's great Yelp: it contains, in capsule form, all that is very right and very wrong with us, and amounts to a complex equation proving that our right and our wrong both proceed out of the same national energy. If the Yelp is a bit rough, off-pitch, and inconsistent in places, God bless him: at least he did it.

As I've worked on this piece, an image has sometimes come to mind of Twain standing outside a jail, and inside the jail is A True American Literature. Twain, wearing, maybe, a top hat, takes a good hard crazy run at it, and knocks the shack down, and A True American Literature is suddenly free to wander about in the world. In the process, Twain's hat is knocked awry, and his nose is broken, and pretty soon a crowd gathers, saying, "Jeez, Mark, your hat's crooked and your nose is broken and your ending stinks and your book seems a little racist"—but damn it, there's that fallen shack, and A True American Literature is now sauntering off into the woods, being eagerly tracked by all those Hungry American Writers, who have included, over the years, Salinger and Ellison and Faulkner and Hemingway and Morrison and Eliot and Bellow and Carver. Twain sacrificed his hat and his nose so the rest of us would have something good to track, and track it we have, all these years, and the tracking of it has helped us, I would argue, confront the very issues that make the book problematic: racism, timidity, denial, our national urge-to-the-genteel.

Twain would like this, I think, this continuing struggle to understand his book. We have not had a writer as devoted to seeking out truth and outing lies. *Huck Finn* is a great book because it tells the truth about the human condition in a way that delights us. It is a great work of our national literature because, more than any book before or since, it locates itself squarely on our National Dilemma, which is: How can anyone be truly free in a country as violent and stupid as ours? The book still lives, because the question does.

BUDDHA BOY

WANT TO SEE A POSSIBLE MIRACLE? NO THANKS, I'M DOING MY TAXES

Last December, I got an e-mail from my editor at *GQ*. A fifteen-year-old boy in Nepal had supposedly been meditating for the past seven months without any food or water. Would I like to look into this?

I went online. The boy's name was Ram Bahadur Bomjon. He was sitting in the roots of a pipal tree near the Indian border. The site was being overrun by pilgrims, thousands a week, who were calling this boy "the new Buddha." He'd twice been bitten by poisonous snakes; both times he'd refused medicine and cured himself via meditation. Skeptics said he was being fed at night behind a curtain, that his guru was building himself a temple, that his parents were building themselves a mansion, that the Maoist rebels, in on the hoax, were raking in tens of thousands of dollars in donations.

I e-mailed my editor back: I was pretty busy, what with the teaching and all, besides which Christmas break was coming up and I hadn't been to the gym once the preceding semester, plus it would be great to, uh, get an early start on my taxes.

Then we embarked on the usual Christmas frenzy, but I couldn't get this boy off my mind. At parties, I noted two general reactions to the statement, *Hey, I heard this kid in Nepal has been meditating uninterruptedly in the jungle for the past seven months without any food or water.*

One type of American—let's call them Realists—will react by making a snack-related joke ("So he finally gets up, and turns out he's sitting on a big pile of Butterfinger wrappers!") and will then explain that it's physically impossible to survive even one week without food or water, much less seven months.

A second type—let's call them Believers—will say, "Wow, that's amazing," they wish they could go to Nepal tomorrow, and will then segue into a story about a transparent spiritual being who once appeared on a friend's pool deck with a message about world peace.

Try it: Go up to the next person you see, and say, *Hey, I heard this kid in Nepal has been meditating uninterruptedly in the jungle for the past seven months without any food or water.*

See what they say.

Or say it to yourself, and see what you say.

What I said, finally, was: This I have to see.

NO NUMBER OF HOT ROLLS
CAN STOP MY MONKEY-MIND

Austrian Airlines is big on hot rolls. Red-clad flight atten-
dants continually tout their hot rolls in the accents of
many nations, including, one feels, nations that haven't
actually been founded yet. ("Hod roolz?" "Hat rahls?"
"Hoot rowls?") The in-flight safety video is troubling: It's
animated and features a Sims-like guy with what looks
like a skinless, skeletal death's-head who keeps turn-
ing to leer at a slim Sims lady who keeps looking away,
alarmed, while trying to get her long legs tucked away
somewhere so Death can't see them. Later she slides
down the emergency slide, holding a Sims baby, Death
still pursuing her.

Ancient Mariner—style, my seatmate, a Kosovar, tells
me about a Serbian paramilitary group called the Black
Hand that left a childhood friend of his on a hillside,
"cut into tiny pieces." During the occupation, he says,
the Serbs often killed babies in front of their parents. He
is kindly, polite, awed by the horrible things he's seen,
grateful that, as an American citizen, he no longer has
to worry about murdered babies or hacked-up friends,
except, it would appear, in memory, constantly.

Story told, he goes off to sleep.

But I can't. I'm too uncomfortable. I'm mad at myself
for eating two roolz during the last Round of Roolz,
roolz that seem to have instantaneously made my pants
tighter. I've already read all my books and magazines,
already stood looking out the little window in the flight-
attendant area, already complimented a severe blond
flight attendant on Austrian Airlines' excellent service,

which elicited an oddly Austrian reaction: She immediately seemed to find me reprehensible and weak.

On the bright side, only six more hours on this plane, then two hours in the Vienna airport and an eight-hour flight to Katmandu.

I decide to close my eyes and sit motionless, to make the time pass.

Somebody slides up their window shade and, feeling the change in light on my eyelids, I am filled with sudden curiosity: Has the shade really been lifted? By someone? Gosh, who was it? What did they look like? What were they trying to accomplish by lifting the shade? I badly want to open my eyes and confirm that a shade has indeed been lifted, by someone, for some purpose. Then I notice a sore patch on the tip of my tongue and feel a strong desire to interrupt my experiment to record the interesting sore-tongue observation in my notebook. Then I begin having Restless Leg Syndrome, Restless Arm Syndrome, and even a little Restless Neck Syndrome. Gosh, am I thirsty. Boy, is my breath going to be bad when this stupid experiment is over. I imagine a waterfall of minty water flowing into my mouth, a waterfall that does not have to be requested via the stern flight attendant but just comes on automatically when I press a button on the overhead console marked Minty Water.

The mind is a machine that is constantly asking: What would I prefer? Close your eyes, refuse to move, and watch what your mind does. What it does is become discontent with That Which Is. A desire arises, you satisfy that desire, and another arises in its place. This wanting and rewanting is an endless cycle for which, turns out, there is already a name: samsara. Samsara is at the heart of the vast human carnival: greed, neurosis, mad ambition, adultery, crimes of passion, the hacking to death of a terrified man on a hillside in the name of A More Pure And Thus Perfect Nation—and all of this takes place because we believe we will be made happy once our desires have been satisfied.

I know this. But still I'm full of desire. I want my legs to stop hurting. I want something to drink. I even kind of want another hot roll.

Seven months, I think? The kid has been sitting there *seven months?*

FORSOOTH, GET ME HITHER TO THE PALACE, AND DON'T SMACK INTO THAT COW

We arrive in Katmandu just before midnight. The city is as dark a city as I've ever seen: no streetlights, no neon, each building lit by one or two small bulbs or a single hanging lantern. It's like a medieval city, smoke-smelling, the buildings leaning into narrow unsquared roads. It's as if the cab has been time-transported back to the age of kings and squalor, and we are making our way through the squalor to the palace, which is the Hyatt. A garbage-eating cow appears in our headlights. We pass a lonely green-lit mod ATM kiosk that looks like it's been dropped in from the future.

The Hyatt lobby is empty except for rows of Buddha statues: a maze with no takers. The Business Center manageress not only has heard of the boy but is also of the opinion that he is being fed by snakes. Their venom, she says, is actually milk to him.

I go to bed, sleep the odd post-trip sleep from which you wake up unsure of where, or who, you are.

In the morning I throw open the curtains, and there is Katmandu: a sprawling Seussian city where prayer flags extend from wacky tower to strange veranda to tilting spire-of-uncertain-purpose. Beyond Seuss City: the Himalayas, pure, Platonically white, the white there was before other colors were invented. In the foreground is the massive, drained, under-repair Hyatt pool, in a field of dead, dry Hyatt grass, and a woman tending to the first of an endless row of shrubs, in a vignette that should be titled "Patience Will Prevail."

I take a walk.

The level of noise, energy, and squalor of Katmandu makes even the poorest section of the most wild-ass American city seem placid and urban-planned. Some guys squat in a trash-strewn field, inexplicably beating the crap out of what looks like purple cotton candy. A woman whose face has been burned or torn off walks past me, running some small errand, an errand made heartbreaking by the way she carries herself, which seems to signify: I'm sure this will be a very good day! Here is a former Pepsi kiosk, now barbed-wired and manned by Nepalese soldiers armed for Maoists; here a Ping-Pong table made of slate, with brick legs. I cross a mythical bleak vacant lot I've seen in dreams, a lot surrounded by odd Nepali brick high-rises like a lake surrounded by cliffs, if the lake were dry and had a squatting, peeing lady in the middle of it. Averting my eyes, I see another woman, with a baby, and teeth that jut, terrifyingly, straight out of her mouth, horizontally, as if her gums had loosened up and she had tilted her teeth out at ninety degrees. She stretches out a hand, jiggles the baby with the other, as if to say: *This baby, these teeth, come on, how are we supposed to live?*

Off to one side of the road is a strange sunken hol-
low—like a shallow basement excavation—filled with
rows of wooden benches on which hundreds of the
dustiest men, women, and children imaginable wait for
something with the sad patience of animals. It's like a
bus station, but there's no road in sight. Several West-
erners huddle near a gate, harried-looking, pissy, admit-
ting people or not. A blind man is expelled from the
lot and lingers by the gate, acting casual, like he was
not just expelled. What's going on here? Three hundred people in a kind of open-air jail, no blind guys
allowed.

I go in, walk through the crowd ("Good mahning
how on you I am fahn!"), and corner a harried Western
woman with several mouth sores.

"What is all this?" I say.

"Soup kitchen," she says.

"For . . . ?" I say.

"Anybody who needs," she says.

And there are many who need: two hundred, three
hundred people a sitting, she says, two sittings a day,
never an empty seat.

This, I think, explains the expelled blind man: He
came too late.

Life is suffering, the Buddha said, by which he did
not mean *Every moment of life is unbearable* but rather
*All happiness/rest/contentment is transient; all appear-
ances of permanence are illusory.*

The faceless woman, the odd-toothed woman, the
dusty elderly people with babies in their laps, waiting for
a meal, the blind guy by the gate, feigning indifference:
In Nepal, it occurs to me, life *is* suffering, nothing esoteric about it.

Then, at the end of a road too narrow for a car,

appears the famous Boudha stupa: huge, pale, glacial, rising out of the surrounding dusty squalor like Hope itself.

WHAT IS A STUPA AND
WHY DO WE NEED ONE?

A stupa is a huge three-dimensional Buddhist prayer aid, usually dome-shaped, often containing some holy relic, a bone or lock of hair from the historical Buddha. This particular stupa has been accreting for many centuries; some accounts date it back to AD 500. It is ringed by a circular street filled with hundreds of circumambulating Buddhist pilgrims from all over Nepal, Tibet, Bhutan, India: wild costumes in every hue of purple, red, and orange; odd piercings and hairstyles. A shop blares a version of the *om mani padme hung* chant over and over, all day. A woman with a goiter the size of a bowling ball gossips with some friends.

The stupa is multileveled, terraced; people circumambulate on each level. Pigeon shadows flee across multiple planar surfaces, along with the shadows of thousands of prayer flags. Barefoot boys lug buckets of yellowish whitewash to the top level and sling these across the surface of the dome, leaving jagged yellow thunderbolts. The only sounds are birdsong and the occasional clanging of a bell and, in the far distance, a power saw.

I do lap after lap, praying for everybody I know. For me, this has been a tough year: A beloved uncle died, my parents' house was destroyed by Katrina, a kindhearted cousin shipped off to Iraq, a car accident left my teenage daughter sobbing by the side of the road on a dark, freezing night, I've found myself loving my wife of eighteen years more than I'd even known you could love another human being—a good thing, except that it involves a terrifying downside: the realization that there must someday come a parting.

Today, at the stupa, it occurs to me that this low-level ambient fear constitutes a decent working definition of the human: A human being is someone who, having lived awhile, becomes terrified and, having become terrified, deeply craves an end to the fear.

All of this—the stupa, the millions of people who have circumambulated it during the hundreds of years since it was built (in Shakespeare's time, while Washington lived, during the Civil War, as Glenn Miller played), the shops, the iconography, the statues, the *tangka* paintings, the chanting, the hundreds of thousands of human lives spent in meditation—all of this began when one man walked into the woods, sat down, and tried to end his fear by doing something purely internal: working on his mind.

As I'm leaving the stupa, a kid drags me into a little room to the side of the main gate. Inside are two massive prayer wheels. He shows me how to spin them. Three laps is recommended for maximum blessing. In one corner sits a midget in monk's robes, praying.

"Lama," my guide says as we pass.

On the second lap, he points out a collection of images of great Buddhist saints, stuck above a small window. Here is the Dalai Lama. Here is Guru Rinpoche, who first brought Buddhism to Tibet. Here is Bomjon, the meditating boy.

The photo shows a boy of about twelve: a chubby

crew-cut smiling little guy, shy but proud, like a Little Leaguer, but instead of a baseball uniform, he's wearing monk's robes.

"Bomjon," I say.

"You are very talent!" says my guide.

BAD AND GETTING WORSE

Back at the Hyatt, I meet Subel, my translator, a kindly, media-savvy twenty-three-year-old who looks like a Nepali Robert Downey Jr. We take a terrifying ride through Katmandu on his motorcycle to a darkened travel agency, where we buy plane tickets by candlelight; Katmandu is under a program called "load shedding," which, in the name of conservation, cuts power to a different part of town every night. The agent processes our tickets sacramentally in the light from three red candles tilted on sheets of newspaper.

Given Nepal's political situation, there's something ominous about the darkened travel agency, a suggestion of bleaker conditions soon to come.

More than ten thousand Nepalis have died in the past ten years in an ongoing war between the monarchy and the Maoists. Over the past three years, the new king has basically canceled the burgeoning but inefficient democracy and seized back all power. A week after I leave, he will arrest opposition leaders, and the most serious attacks yet on Katmandu will take place.

Over dinner, Subel (like some prerevolutionary Russian intellectual, a Herzen or Belinsky, personally offended by the cruelty of his government) gets tears in his eyes telling me about a twenty-year-old Nepali woman who died in a distant airport, unable to get to the Katmandu hospital because the inefficient airline canceled all flights for three days straight; tells about the arrogant Nepali soldiers who pulled over two friends of his, singers, and made them sing on the street as the soldiers laughed at them. He doesn't want to ever leave Nepal, he says, unless in doing so he can acquire a useful skill and come back and "make some differences."

The country is scared, wired, suffering, dreading an imminent explosion that will take a catastrophically poor country and turn it into a catastrophically poor country in a state of civil war. In Katmandu it seems everybody knows about the meditating boy, follows news of him avidly, believes he's doing what he's said to be doing, and wishes him luck. They feel him, you sense, as a kind of savior-from-within, a radical new solution to festering old problems. Political pragmatism exhausted, they're looking for something, anything, to save them.

A friend of Subel's tells me he hopes the meditating boy will do "something good for this country," meaning, to my ear, *something good for this poor, beaten-down country, which I dearly love.*

TO GET THERE, HEAD IN THE DIRECTION OF POOR

Next morning we fly to the southern village of Simra in a submarine-like plane that has, for a sun visor, a piece of newspaper taped to the windshield. The seats are webbed and metal-framed like lawn chairs, the floor made of carpetless dented metal. We pass, barely, over one-room farmhouses perched atop cartoonishly steep mountains, entire spreads consisting of just a postage-stamp-sized green terrace dug out of a gray mountainside. From Simra we take a jeep to Birgunj and spend a restless night in a Gogolian hotel where the bathroom lights buzz even when off, and I am perplexed by a mysterious panel of seven switches that never seem to control the same light twice.

Next morning we're off to see the boy.

We head back through Simra by minivan and then beyond, through a swirl of the maddest poverty: Girls plod out of deep woods with stacks of huge leaves on their backs to feed some animal; a woman squats to piss, yards away from a muddy pond where another woman draws water; men pound metal things with other metal things; dirty kids are sniffed by dirty dogs as dogs and kids stand in trash.

After a couple of hours, we pull off into a kind of gravel staging area overhung with red welcome banners. On a large billboard—the only one I've seen all morning—a personified condom gives an enraptured young couple some advice out of its jauntily tilted receptacle tip: "Please, enjoy safe sex!"

"Is this it?" I say.

"This is it," Subel says.

BUT STILL WE ARE NOT THERE

Beyond the staging area, the road goes single-vehicle, double-rutted. I try taking notes, but the road is too bumpy. *CRWLFF!* I write, *FHWUED??*

The jungle gets denser; a dry riverbed on the right disappears into the trees. Finally, we reach a kind of minivillage of crude wooden stalls. Boy-related postcards and framed photos and pamphlets are for sale, along with flowers and scarves to present as offerings. We leave the van and walk along a dirt road. Pilgrim-related garbage lines the ditches on either side. A TV on a rickety roadside table blares a Bollywood video: a woman so sexy she captivates a shipful of genial sailors. At a climactic moment, she drops backward into a giant cup of tea, causing a blind man to lose his treasured bur-lap sack.

A mile farther on, we leave our shoes in a kind of Shoe Corral, take a narrow path worn smooth by tens of thousands of pilgrim feet. The path passes through the roots of a large pipal tree hung with pictures of the boy. A quarter mile more and we reach a tree-posted sign in Nepali, requesting quiet and forbidding flash photogra-phy, especially flash photography aimed at the meditat-ing boy. Beyond the sign, seven or eight recently arrived pilgrims stand at a gate in a barbed-wire fence, craning to see the boy while stuffing small bills into a wooden donation box mounted on the fence.

Though I can't see him from here, he's *there*, right over there somewhere, maybe five hundred feet away, in that exact cluster of trees.

I step through the pilgrims, to the fence, and look inside.

WHAT I EXPECT TO SEE, BASED ON WHAT I'VE READ

Online accounts say that at night a curtain is drawn around the boy. This is presumably how he's being fed: at night, behind the curtain. So I expect to see the drawn-back curtain hanging from . . . what? The tree itself? Or maybe they've built some kind of structure into the tree: an adjacent room, a kind of backstage area—a place where his followers hang out and keep the food they're sneaking him at night.

In my projection of it, the site resembles the only large-capacity outdoor venue I'm familiar with: a rock concert, with the boy at center stage.

A SLIGHT REWIND, AND WHAT
I ACTUALLY SEE

I step through the pilgrims, to the fence, and look inside.

The first impression is zoolike. You are looking into an Enclosure. Inside the Enclosure are dozens of smallish pipal trees festooned with a startling density of prayer flags (red, green, yellow, many faded to white from the sun and rain). This Enclosure also has a vaguely military feel: something recently and hastily constructed, with security in mind.

I scan the Enclosure, looking for That Which Is Enclosed. Nothing. I look closer, focusing on three or four larger trees that, unlike the smaller trees, have the characteristic flaring pipal roots. This too feels zoolike: the scanning, the rescanning, the sudden sense of Ah, *there* he is!

Because there he is.

At this distance (about two hundred feet), it's hard to distinguish where the boy's body ends and the tree roots begin. I can make out his black hair, one arm, one shoulder.

The effect is now oddly crèche-like. You are glimpsing an ancient vignette that will someday become mythic but that for now is occurring in real time, human-scaled, warts and all: small, sloppy concrete blobs at the base of the fence posts; an abandoned tree-house-like plat-form near the boy's tree; a red plastic chair midway between the fence I'm standing at, and a second, inner fence.

No secret tree-adjacent room.

No curtain, and nowhere to hang a curtain, although there is a kind of prayer-flag sleeve about ten feet above the boy's head that could conceivably be slid down at night.

There's nobody inside the Enclosure but the boy.

And a young monk standing near the gate. The monk's bangs appear bowl-cut. He's wearing a St. Francis–evoking robe. There is something striking about him, an odd spiri-tual intensity/charisma. He appears very young and very old at the same time. There is a suggestion of the extrater-restrial about his head-body ratio, his posture, his quality of birdlike concentration.

Between the gate and the inner fence is a wide dirt path leading up to where the boy is sitting. Only digni-taries and journalists are allowed inside the Enclosure. Subel has assured me we'll be able to get in.

I sit on a log. What I'll do is hang out here for an hour or so, get my bearings, take a few notes on the general site layout, and—

"Okay, man," Subel says tersely. "We go in now."

"Now?" I say.

"Uh, if you want to go in?" Subel says. "Now is it."

Meaning: Now or never, bro. I just barely talked you in.

The crowd parts. Some Village Guy—head of a Vil-lage Committee formed to maintain the site and provide security for the boy—unlocks the gate. The young monk looks me over. He's not suspicious exactly; protective, maybe. He makes me feel (or I make me feel) that I'm disturbing the boy for frivolous reasons, like the embodiment of Western Triviality, a field rep for the Society of International Travel Voyeurs.

We step inside, followed by a gray-haired lama in purple robes. The lama and the young monk start down a wide path that leads to the inner fence, ending directly in front of, and about fifty feet away from, the boy.

Subel and I follow.

My mouth is dry, and I have a sudden feeling of gratitude/reverence/terror. What a privilege. Oh God, I have somehow underestimated the gravity of this place and moment. I am potentially at a great religious site, in the original, mythic time: at Christ's manger, say, with Shakyamuni at Bodh Gaya, watching Moses come down from the Mount. I don't want to go any farther, actually. We're in the boy's sight line now, if somebody with eyes closed can be said to have a sight line, closing fast, walking directly at him. It's quieter and tenser than I could have imagined. We are walking down the aisle of a silent church toward a stern, judging priest.

We reach the inner fence: as far as anyone is allowed to go.

At this distance, I can really see him. His quality of nonmotion is startling. His head doesn't move. His arms, hands, don't move. Nothing moves. His chest does not constrict/expand with breathing. He could be dead. He could be carved from the same wood as the tree. He is thinner than in the photos; that is, his one exposed arm is thinner. Thinner but not emaciated. He still has good muscle tone. Dust is on everything. His dusty hair has grown past the tip of his nose. His hair is like a helmet.

He wears a sleeveless brown garment. His hands are in one of the mudras in which the Buddha's hands are traditionally depicted. He is absolutely beautiful: beautiful as the central part of this crèche-like, timeless vignette, beautiful in his devotion. I feel a stab of something for him. Allegiance? Pity? Urge-to-Protect? My heart rate is going through the roof.

The gray-haired lama, off to my right, drops, does three quick prostrations: a Buddhist sign of respect, a way of reminding oneself of the illuminated nature of all beings, performed in the presence of spiritually advanced beings in whom this illuminated nature is readily apparent.

The lama begins his second prostration. *Me too*, I mutter, and down I go. Dropping, I think I glimpse the boy's hand move. Is he signaling me? Does he recognize, in me, something special? Has he been, you know, kind of *waiting* for me? In the midst of my final prostration, I realize: His hand didn't move, dumb ass. It was wishful thinking. It was ego, nimrod: The boy doesn't move for seven months but can't help but move when George arrives, since George is George and has always been George, something very George-special?

My face is flushed from the prostrations and the effort of neurotic self-flagellation.

The gray-haired lama takes off at a fast walk, circumambulating the boy clockwise on a path that runs on this side of the inner fence.

The young monk says something to Subel, who tells me it's time to take my photo. My photo? I have a camera but don't want to risk disturbing the boy with the digital shutter sound. Plus, I don't know how to turn off the flash, so I will be, at close range, taking a flash photo directly into the boy's sight line, the one thing explicitly prohibited by that sign back there.

"You have to," Subel says. "That's how they know you're a journalist."

I hold up my notebook. Maybe I could just take some notes?

"They're simple people, man," he says. "You have to take a photo."

I set the camera to video mode (no flash involved), pan back and forth across the strangely beautiful Enclosure, zoom in on the boy.

It's one thing to imagine seven months of nonmotion, but to see, in person, even ten minutes of such utter nonmotion is stunning. I think, Has he really been sitting like that since May? *May?* All through the London bombings, the Cairo bombings, the unmasking of Deep Throat, Katrina, the Israeli withdrawal from Gaza, the Lynndie England trial, the Bali bombing, the Kashmir earthquake, the Paris riots, the White Sox World Series victory, the NYC transit strike, through every thought and purchase and self-recrimination of the entire Christmas season?

Suddenly, the question of his not eating seems almost beside the point.

The young monk says that if we like, we may now do a circumambulation. Meaning: Time's up.

We start off, the young monk accompanying us.

His name, he says, is Prem.

WHAT WE LEARN FROM PREM

Prem grew up with the boy; they're distant cousins, but he characterizes them as "more friends than relatives."

They became monks at the same time, just after fourth grade. A couple of years ago, they traveled together to Lumbini, the birthplace of the Buddha, for a ten-day Buddhist ceremony being led by a renowned teacher from Dehra Dun, India. There the boy was invited to undertake a three-year retreat at this lama's monastery.

But after one year, the boy left the monastery—*fled* is the verb Prem uses—with just the clothes on his back. Prem doesn't know why. Nobody does. The boy came home briefly, vanished again, after a dream in which a god appeared to him and told him that if he didn't leave home he would die. His distraught family found him under this tree, rarely speaking, refusing food. The family and the villagers were mortified, embarrassed, demanded he stop. He was teased, poked with sticks, tempted with food, but still refused to eat. Three months into his meditation, he called for Prem, asked him to manage the site, minimize the noise. Prem is now his main attendant, here every day from early morning until dusk.

"Who is inside the Enclosure with him at night?" I ask.

"Nobody," Prem says.

Prem shows us an area just inside the fence where, per the boy's request, Prem performs Buddhist rituals: a puja table, incense pots, texts.

It was just here, he tells us, that the first snake, crawling in, got stuck under the fence. The monks assisting at the time couldn't kill it, for religious reasons, and were struggling inefficiently to free it. Finally, the boy got up from his meditation, walked over, and freed the snake. As he did so, the snake lunged up and bit him.

"What kind of snake was it?" I ask, trying to be journalistic.

"It was . . . a big jungle snake," Subel translates.

"Ah," I say.

The snakes, Prem says, were "arrows" sent by older lamas, jealous because they'd practiced all their lives and hadn't attained this level of realization.

I ask about the boy's meditation practice. What exactly is he doing? Does Prem know?

Prem hesitates, says something to Subel in a softer voice.

"His belief is, this boy is God," Subel says. "God has come to earth in the form of this boy."

I look at Prem. He looks at me. In his eyes, I see that he knows this statement sounds a little wacky. I try, with my eyes, to communicate my basic acceptance of the possibility.

We have a moment.

Does the boy ever move or adjust his posture?

Prem smiles for the first time, laughs even. The sense is: Ha, very funny, believe me, he *never* moves. People accuse us all the time, he says. They say, This is not a boy, it is a statue, a dummy, something carved from clay.

What was the boy like as a cousin, as a friend?

A good boy. Very sweet-hearted. Never cursed. Did not drink alcohol or eat meat.

He would always smile first, then speak.

A BRIEF CHAT WITH THE MAN

Back near the Shoe Corral, we talk with the Village Guy. He seems frazzled, overworked, cognizant of the fact that anybody with a lick of sense would suspect him and the Committee of being at the heart of any hoax, anxious to address such concerns in a straightforward way. He reminds me of one of my down-to-earth Chicago uncles, if one of my Chicago uncles suddenly found himself neglecting everything else in his life to tend to a miracle. His attitude seems to be: *Why should I lie? You think I'm enjoying this? You want to take over?* So far the Committee has collected approximately 445,000 rupees (about $6,500). A portion of this is used for site maintenance and the small salaries of eighteen volunteers; the rest is being held in a bank for the boy.

Something occurs to me: It's one thing to, from afar, project a scheming, greedy group of villagers in a faraway land, but when you actually get to the land, you see that, before they were scheming, they had intact, in-place lives, lives that did not involve scheming. They were fathers, husbands, grandfathers, keepers-of-backyard-gardens, local merchants. They had reputations. For someone to risk these preexisting lives (lives which are, in this case, small, impoverished, precarious) would take a considerable level of forethought, risk, and diabolical organization. Imagine that first meeting: *Okay, so what we'll do is get a kid to pretend to be meditating and not eating, then sneak him food and water and get the word out internationally, and before long—bingo—we've got six grand in the bank! Everyone in agreement? Ready? Let's go!*

WELCOME, WELCOME, PLEASE LEAVE AT ONCE

After lunch, bound for the boy's village, we cross a dry riverbed of coarse gray sand, like cremated ashes, into which some men are sinking a water well.

When a fairy tale says, *He left his village and set out*

to seek his fortune, this is the village you might imagine the hero leaving: a cluster of huts along a dirt track.
Mustard and corn growing on rounded slopes, higher
than your head. Kids racing in dust clouds behind the
minivan, baby chicks skittering off into high weeds, as if
dropping out of the children's clothes.

The boy's mother is home but unhappy to see me. I
would describe her reaction as a wince, if a wince could
be accomplished without a change of facial expression:
As Subel introduces me, she undergoes a kind of full-
body stiffening, then plucks three glasses off a tray with
the fingers of one hand and disappears brusquely inside
the house.

So much for that, I think.

But then a little girl comes out with the three glasses,
now full of tea. The mother sits, submitting to torture
in the name of politeness. She's an older woman, pretty,
with a nose ring, answers my questions without ever once
looking at me.

When he was born, he didn't cry the way other babies
do. Instead, he made a different kind of sound, a sound
she describes as a sharp scream.

He kind of shouted out, she says.

As a child, he was totally different from her other
children. He was a loner, always wandering off on his
own. When people would scold or bully him, he would
just smile. When he came back from the monastery in
India, his speech patterns had changed: If he kept to
small sentences he was fine, but when he tried to talk in
longer sentences he would get anxious and agitated and
descend into gibberish; no one could understand him.
She thought maybe some kind of curse had been put on
him by the lama he'd fled. But now she understands: He

was going through a profound change. The main problem at this point, she says, is the noise. He can't concentrate on his meditation. They have gone so far as to outlaw one group from coming to the site, a sect from a particular part of the Tarai, known for being loud. (Subel later relays a common slur about this group: You can't tell if they're laughing or screaming in agony.)

All of this is happening for a reason, she says. There is a God in him that is helping him feed himself. She sits quietly, grieved, flies landing on her face, waiting for this to be over.

She puts me in mind, of course, of the Virgin Mary: a simple countrywoman, mother of a son who appears in a time of historical crisis representing a solution and a hope above politics.

We walk back to the van, followed by the flock of kids, who still seem to be miraculously sprouting baby chicks.

Our plan is: Go back to the hotel, get some rest. Come back tomorrow, spend the night, see if some kind of Secret Eating is taking place.

It's misty, getting cold. There are open fires along the road, and local governments are distributing free firewood, concerned that people will freeze to death tonight in the countryside.

And they do. During this night, over a hundred people die of exposure across India, Nepal, and Bangladesh, including one old man in this district. Temperatures in Delhi reach their coldest recorded levels in over seventy years.

And tomorrow night, the driver tells us, it's going to be even colder.

THE LONGEST NIGHT IN HISTORY,
PART I: THIS WILL BE SO GREAT!

Next evening the driver drops us at the Shoe Corral.

He'll return tomorrow morning at eight.

Nearby is a kind of crude tent: four trees hacked into tent poles, with what looks like a parachute draped over them. This is the Committee Tent, where volunteer members of the Committee stay overnight to provide security. But tonight there's no Committee, just the boy's brother and a friend. Though not expecting us, they have no objection to our staying. Three lamas from Eastern Nepal will also be here, meditating all night. Will we need mats? Do I want to sleep near the lamas down by the gate, or up here at the tent near the fire?

We leave our shoes at the tent. The lamas are seated in front of the gate on a single mat, canoe-style. The brother puts my mat ten feet or so behind them, placing it carefully so leaf moisture won't fall on me.

Prem has left for the night. The brother checks the padlock on the gate. Sitting, I can't see the boy, but if I crane around the monks, I can see his tree. I'm wearing thermal long johns under a pair of khaki pants, a long-sleeve thermal undershirt, a sweater, and a sleeveless down vest.

This won't be bad, I think.

It gets dark fast. A big moon rises, just short of full. The brother and his pal hiss angrily back and forth, then launch off on a perimeter check, their flashlight bobbing away in the dark.

From inside the Enclosure, or maybe the far side of it, I hear what sounds like a cough. Sound is traveling strangely. Was that the boy? Did the boy just cough? To note this possible cough in my notebook, I devise a system: I take out my mini-flashlight, mute the light with my hand, so as not to disturb the boy, record the time, make my note.

At 7:20, oddly, a car alarm goes off. How many cars in deep rural Nepal have alarms? It goes on and on. Finally it dawns on me, when the car alarm moves to a different tree, that the car alarm is a bird.

The Car-Alarm Bird of Southern Nepal keeps it up for ten minutes, then falls silent for the rest of the night.

In this quiet, even the slightest posture adjustment is deafening. If a tiny breeze picks up, you notice. If a drop of moisture falls, you jump. So when one of the lamas stands up and goes to the fence, it's a major event. The other lamas whisper, point excitedly. The first lama paces back to me, gestures by touching his fingers to his forehead and flinging something outward. I don't get it. He has a headache? His head is really sweating? He motions for me to return with him. Soon I'm sitting canoe-style between Lama One and Lama Two. I can hear Lama One mumbling mantras under his breath. Suddenly he turns to me, again makes the gesture, points into the Enclosure. I get it now: The gesture means, *Look, there is something emanating from the boy's forehead!*

Do I see it?

Actually, I do: Vivid red and blue lights (like flares) are hovering, drifting up from approximately where the boy is sitting, as if borne upward on an impossibly light updraft.

What the heck, I think. My face goes hot. Is this what a miracle looks like, feels like, in real time? I close my eyes, open them. The lights are still drifting up.

A noise begins, a steady drumlike thumping from inside the Enclosure, like an impossibly loud heartbeat.

For several concept-free seconds, it's just: colored up-floating lights and the boy's amplified heartbeat.

I look through the binoculars. Yes, red and blue sparks, yep, and now, wow, green. And orange. Then suddenly, they're all orange. They look—actually, they look like orange cinders. Like orange cinders floating up from a fire. A campfire, say. I lower the binoculars. Seen with the naked eye, the sparks look to be coming not from inside the Enclosure but from just beyond it. Slowly, a campfire resolves itself in the distance. The heartbeat becomes syncopated. The heartbeat is coming from off to my right and behind me and is actually, I can now tell, a drum, from a village out in the jungle.

I stand up, go to the gate. That, I think, is a campfire. I've never seen, it's true, red/blue/green cinders, but still, that is, I am almost positive, a campfire. I'm embarrassed on the boy's behalf for his motley, boisterous, easily excited entourage.

But maybe, part of me protests, this is how a miracle happens?

Another part answers: It has all the marks of a Sunday school.

I return to my assigned spot, resolve to ignore all future faux-excitement, and just watch.

THE LONGEST NIGHT IN HISTORY, PART II: COLD, COLDER, UNBEARABLY COLD

At 8:30, I take my winter hat and gloves from my pack. Abruptly the lamas rise and exit in a group. What, I think, the lamas are chickening out? I'm tougher than the lamas? Soon they return, laden with mattresses and fat sleeping rolls and plump pillows. What, I think, the lamas are incredibly well prepared for what is shaping up to be a damn cold night?

Subel goes back to the Committee Tent to sit by the fire.

Now it's just me and the snoring, sleep-moaning lamas.

From near the source of the drumming, I suddenly hear dozens of barking dogs. The drum patterns morph into Native American patterns from old Westerns, as if what they're doing over in that village is planning to attack and overrun our little outpost here, using their constantly barking attack dogs.

Before long the dogs and drums fade and I'm lapsing into odd exhausted waking dreams: The boy sticks a pole into my chest, which is made of fiberboard, so the pole goes in easily and painlessly. *Don't go for the heart,* he says. I don't get it. *Should I write about you?* I ask. *Sure,* he says, *go ahead, just tell the truth, doubts and contradictions and all. I don't mind.*

Soon my legs and feet are freezing. I take my socks out of my pocket and put them on. The vest/sweater combo is keeping my torso warm, but my neck and legs are becoming problematic. I drape a pair of dirty sweatpants around my neck, take out my coat (a shell that's supposed to have a fleece lining, which I've somehow managed to lose), arrange it over my legs. Subel returns from the fire and stretches out behind me, trying to sleep. I think of him back there: no socks, just a flannel shirt and a light windbreaker. I have an emergency blanket in my pack, a tinfoilish thing in a small cardboard box. I throw it back to him, he unrolls it for what seems like hours: the noisiest thing I've ever heard.

"Am I being too loud?" he asks sweetly.

By 10:30, he's asleep. I'm fading fast. The dogs sound distant, gooselike. The drummer seems tired. I try to feel the boy sitting out there, and really I can't. How are you doing this? I think. Forget eating, how do you *sit* so long? My back hurts, my legs hurt, the deep soreness in my ass seems to connote Permanent Damage.

At 10:58, a jet passes overhead, bound for Katmandu.

At 11:05, I take the dirty sweatpants from around my neck, stand up, put them on over my khakis. I put the coat/shell on, drawstring it tight, tuck my chin down, so none of my face is exposed. With a rush of happiness, I remember there are two more dirty pairs of pants in my pack! I drape them like blankets over my legs and feet. What else do I have? Two pairs of dirty underwear, which I briefly consider putting on my head.

By 11:22, I can see my breath.

Even in my socks, my feet are freezing. I sit still; any move may cause an increase in Coldness, and any increased Coldness is, at this point, unacceptable. I remember a certain yoga move that involves tightening the rectum to get a heat tingle to surge up the spine, and do this, and it feels better, but not better enough to justify the exhausting rectal flexing.

At 11:55, dozing off, I wake to the sound of a woman's voice, possibly my wife, shouting my name from near the Committee Tent.

Time slows way down. I wait and wait to check my watch. Three hours go by, slow, torturous hours. It is now, I calculate, around three in the morning. Excellent: Next will come predawn, then dawn, then the minivan, the hotel, America. As a special treat, I allow myself to check my watch.

It's 12:10. Fifteen minutes—fifteen minutes?—have passed since my wife called my name. Dammit, shit! I find myself in the strange position of being angry at Time.

Subel stirs, gets up, says he's going back to the tent: His feet are too cold.

I take out the flashlight, carefully write: *If it gets colder than this I'm fucked.*

It gets colder.

Soon I'm making no effort to stay awake or, ha ha, meditate: just trying not to freak out, because if I freak out and flee into the Nepali darkness, it will still be freezing and I'll still have eight hours to wait (eight hours? Christ!) before the minivan returns.

At 12:15, time officially stops. My current posture (sitting up cross-legged) becomes untenable. I can't help it. I fall over on my side. This is going to invalidate the whole idea of: Stay up all night, confirm no Overnight Feeding. Oh, fuck that, I think, have a feast, I don't care. The ground is hard and cold through the thin mat. I ball the dirty pants up around my frozen feet. The drums start again, accompanied by the inexplicable smell of burning rubber. Wherefore burning rubber? I can't figure it.

It starts to rain.

To say I fall asleep would be inaccurate. It's more like I pass out: unwilled, involuntary, unstoppable. Out I go, totally, like a wino on whom a clothes hamper has exploded.

I would characterize the quality of my sleep as: terrified/defiant. I am think-dreaming: Hypothermia! People died out here last night, people who were probably wrapped in blankets. People are probably dying right now. This is serious; try and wake up, really.

I won't wake up, I won't, I answer myself. Because if I wake up, I'll be back where I was before, trapped in that freezing endless torment of a night.

But finally I do wake up, with a start, shivering, colder than I've ever been in my life. I struggle back to a sitting position, find my flashlight, groggily check the time.

It's 1:20.

I've slept an hour.

Shit shit shit, the night is still young.

It starts to rain harder. The flashlight makes a little hiss-pop and goes out—possibly, it occurs to me, the boy's way of saying: Lights out.

Looking into the darkness, I think: Still there? Through all of this, and much more, so many other intolerable nights, before I even knew you existed? If Snake One bit you on a night like this, did you hear it coming? Did you think of bolting, screaming out, calling for your mother?

Poor kid is just sitting in the dark all alone. Tonight, anyway, nobody seems to have the slightest interest in feeding him.

Something powerful starts to dawn on me.

No one has entered the Enclosure all night. After a couple of early checks, the brother and his pal hightailed it back to the Committee Tent. The only entry, the front gate, has been locked since we arrived.

The fact that the Powers That Be (tonight, just the brother and his pal) let us spend the night with no advance notice argues against the existence of a Secret Feeding Plan, because any such Plan would therefore constantly be at the mercy of Drop-Ins, i.e., would have to be aborted anytime anyone showed up to spend the night. There could theoretically be days in a row, weeks even, when it would be impossible to perform the food sneakage.

A suave, logical Devil's Advocate arrives in my mind.

Come on, think aggressively, he says. Don't be a sucker. Is there any possible way they can be sneaking him food?

They could theoretically, I answer, be hiding food in the woods and bringing it in over the fence at a position far from the gate.

Could a person get over that fence without making any noise? he says.

I don't think so, I say. I can hear it anytime anyone leaves the tent, even to pee. And besides, how does an earnest hyperreligious monk who dreams of a god telling him to flee his home become a boy who willingly and sneakily accepts food and water when he has publicly forsworn these?

Good point, says the Devil's Advocate.

Doesn't ring true, I say.

No, it doesn't, the Devil's Advocate says, and fades away.

THE LONGEST NIGHT IN HISTORY, PART III: FURTHER CRAZY TALK IN THE NIGHT AS MY ENERGY DROPS TO SCARY LEVELS

No light appears in the distance to signal dawn, not at all; it just keeps getting darker. I'm shivering, desperate for the paradise of that sad little gray van. I'll put my feet up on the seat, have the driver crank up the heat! We'll stop for tea; I'll pour the tea down my freezing three pairs of pants! I hallucinate a Georgia O'Keeffe flower that opens and closes in megaslow motion while changing colors. I walk downhill into some sacred cave, part of a line of chanting Eastern Holy Men. One of the Holy Men asks a ponderous Zen question, which I answer in a comedian voice via some kind of fart joke. A laugh track sounds in my mind. The Holy Men are not amused. The boy intervenes: *That is his way of being profound*, he says, *leave him alone.*

I'm so tired, says the Devil's Advocate, who has now come back.

Oh God, me too, I say.

Finally, I give up on getting comfortable, and this seems to help. It's a strange thing, staying up all night in the jungle to see if a teenager pulls a fast one via eating. The pain I am feeling at every sensor is making me kind of giddy. Being beyond tired, beyond cold, completely stripped of control, I'm finding, has the effect of clearing the mind.

You know that feeling at the end of the day, when the anxiety of that-which-I-must-do falls away and, for maybe the first time that day, you see, with some clarity, the people you love and the ways you have, during that day, slightly ignored them, turned away from them to get back to what you were doing, blurted out some mildly hurtful thing, projected, instead of the deep love you really feel, a surge of defensiveness or self-protection or suspicion? That moment when you think, Oh God, what have I done with this day? And what am I doing with my life? And how must I change to avoid catastrophic end-of-life regrets?

I feel like that now: tired of the Me I've always been, tired of making the same mistakes, repetitively stumbling after the same small ego strokes, being caught in the same loops of anxiety and defensiveness. At the end of my life, I know I won't be wishing I'd held more back, been less effusive, more often stood on ceremony, forgiven less, spent more days oblivious to the secret wishes and fears of the people around me. So what is stopping me from stepping outside my habitual crap?

My mind, my limited mind.

The story of life is the story of the same basic mind readdressing the same problems in the same already discredited ways. First order of business: Feed the trap. Work the hours to feed the trap. Having fed the trap, shit, piss, preparing to again feed the trap. Because it is your trap, defend it at all costs.

Because we feel ourselves first and foremost as physical beings, the physical comes to dominate us: Beloved uncles die, parents are displaced, cousins go to war, children suffer misfortune, love becomes a trap. The deeper in you go, the more it hurts to get out. Disaster (sickness, death, loss) is guaranteed and in fact is already en route, and when it comes, it hurts and may even destroy us.

We fight this by making ourselves less vulnerable, mastering the physical, becoming richer, making bigger safety nets, safer cars, better medicines.

But it's nowhere near enough.

What if the boy is making this fight in a new way, by struggling against the thousands-of-years-old usage patterns of the brain? What if he is the first of a new breed—or the most recent manifestation of an occasionally appearing breed—sent to show us something new about ourselves, a new way our bodies and minds can work?

Could it be? Could it?

Part of me wants to hop the outer fence, hop the inner fence, sit knee to knee with him, demand to know what the hell is going on.

I get up, but just to take a piss. It's so dark I can't tell when I've left the trail. There are dim shapes on the ground, but I can't tell if they're holes, shrubs, or shadows. I think of snakes. I think: Bring them on. Then I think: Hoo boy, no no, don't bring them on. I try to get deep enough into the woods that nobody will, tomorrow, step in my piss. When I do go, it's Niagara-esque, so loud the boy must hear it, if in fact he's still hearing things.

Sorry, sorry, I think, I just really had to go.

I look up into the vast Nepali sky. Night, I conclude, is a very long thing. Is he suffering in there as much as I'm suffering out here? I wonder.

If so, then what he's doing is a monumental, insane feat of willpower.

If not, it's something even stranger.

THE LONGEST NIGHT IN HISTORY, PART IV: I DON'T DIE

Hours later, at a moment that (in the quality of light, a slight shift in the ambient sound) feels like the Beginning of the Beginning of Morning—the colored lights appear again.

I struggle to the fence, trying not to tread upon any sleeping lamas. Scattered across the ground inside the Enclosure are thousands of snowflakelike silverish glittering flecks. I perform a test, developed back in my acid days: Are the flecks also on my hands? They are. Are they still visible when I close my eyes? They are. Therefore they are an optical illusion, albeit one I have never had before or heard of anyone else ever having.

Oh man, I think, I have no idea what's going on here. The line between miracle and hallucination is all but gone. I am so tired. The center is not . . . What is it the center is sometimes said not to do? Hanging? Having? The center are not hanging.

The lights go white, then orange. Definitely orange. I visually compare this new orange bulk of light to the orange bulk of light I know is the fire back at the Committee Tent.

Again I conclude that the miracle is a campfire.

And yet.

And yet.

Undeniably, over an indefinite period of time, during which time continues not to pass, it gets lighter. The canoeful of lamas rises up, confers briefly, rushes off on a good-morning circumambulation.

I go to the fence.

The sun comes up.

The boy is revealed, sitting, still sitting, in exactly the same position as when I last saw him, at sundown. How did you do it, I think, in your thin sleeveless garment? All night bare to the cold, matless on the cold ground, in full lotus: no coat, no gloves, no socks, no hope of an early-morning rescue.

It seems impossible he's not dead. He looks made of stone, utterly motionless, as impervious to the night as the tree he appears to be part of. Can I see his breath? I can't. Does his chest expand and contract? It doesn't, not that I can see.

Because this night was hard for me, part of me expects it was hard for him and won't be surprised if he stands up and announces he's quitting.

But then I remember he's already spent on the order of two hundred nights out here.

I take what I know will be my last look at him, hoping for . . . I'm not sure what. Some indication that he's alive, that he's operating within the same physical constraints as I am: an adjustment of posture, a clearing of the throat, a weary sigh.

Nothing.

I feel, to gravely understate it, the monumental distance between his abilities and mine.

Pilgrims begin arriving. They step to the fence, gape in wonder, dash off along the circular path, chatting loudly, speculating on what he's doing and why he's doing it.

In short, a new day begins.

I rejoin Subel at the Committee Tent.

"I salute you," he says.

"I salute you," I say.

Both of us are in a state of sleep-deprived paranoia. It has separately occurred to us that the boy must be dead or in a coma. When Subel brought this up last night at the fire, the brother's only explanation was that since the boy sits leaning slightly forward, if he does die, he'll topple forward. Subel asks me how long it takes a body to decay. We try to remember: Didn't Prem tell us that he goes to the ditch every morning and checks to make sure the boy is breathing?

We are relatively sure he did.

The family, Subel tells me, desperate to prove that this is real, is livid with the government and the media for not arranging appropriate scientific tests. They will do anything to help; their only condition is that the boy not be touched, since this would interfere with his meditation.

We experience the deep delight of putting our shoes on again. At one of the stalls, we stop for tea. We have breakfast at another. We are escaped from the boy, from his asceticism, like guilty holidaymakers, lowering ourselves back into the deliriously physical, the realm where any discomfort is instantly reckoned with.

We drive back to Birgunj. Subel is thoughtful: He came out here doubting this boy, he says, but now thinks there is something there, the boy seems to have some power. . . .

An early-morning fog is on everything. In the heavy traffic, we have several gravel-crunching close calls. But soon enough, we're sleeping through even these.

Back at the hotel, under every blanket I can find, including the reclaimed emergency blanket, I sleep all afternoon, a deep, dream-drenched sleep: more O'Keeffe flowers; more secret communiqués from the boy; finally, a series of impossibly detailed *tangka*-like patterns in reds and yellows, constituting themselves into being from right to left. The patterns are intricate, encoded, terrifying in their complexity, full of love and challenge and cocky intelligence, beautiful and original in ways I wouldn't have believed possible if I weren't seeing it right in front of me, with my own eyes.

EPILOGUE: WHEREVER YOU ARE, I WISH YOU WELL

Two months later, on March 11, 2006, I get an e-mail from Subel: "A very bad thing has happened. The

Buddha Boy suddenly vanished last night. He is not there anymore. There are so many reports and stories, but nothing is certain. He might have shifted to another location, but no one knows. The Committee has no idea where he might have gone. They have denied the possibility that he has been abducted. They are all, including the police and the local administration, looking for the boy."

I'm kind of blown away by this. It occurs to me that I've developed a faith in this boy, a confidence that, years from now, he'll have just finished his sitting, and I'll be able to come back to Nepal and ask him what he learned, what I should do, what we all should do, based on what he's learned.

Over the next week, more rumors: The fence was cut. His clothes were left under the tree. He was seen by a villager, walking slowly into the jungle. The boy turned, placed his hands together in greeting, continued. Hundreds of people were out searching for him but had so far found nothing.

Then, on March 20, the BBC reported that the boy had briefly reappeared for a secret meeting with the Chairman of the Village Committee. He said he was going into hiding and would reappear again in six years. He asked that monks perform purification prayers at the spot of his meditation. He was quoted as saying, "I left because there is no peace here. Tell my parents not to worry."

So it's a mystery, even more than it was a mystery before, when it was already pretty damn mysterious.

But I imagine him the night of his escape, making his way through the woods in the moonlight, weak on his feet from months of fasting and sitting, his eyes really open for the first time since May. The world, the beautiful world, is fleeing past, and he's seeing it in a way we can't imagine. He's come so far and is desperate to get somewhere beyond the reach of the world, so he can finish what he's started.

He hasn't eaten in months, and isn't hungry.

MANIFESTO

Now it can be told.

Last Thursday, my organization, People Reluctant To Kill For An Abstraction (PRKA), orchestrated an overwhelming show of force around the globe.

At precisely nine in the morning, working with focus and stealth, our entire membership succeeded in simultaneously beheading no one. At nine thirty, we embarked upon Phase II, during which our entire membership simultaneously did not force a single man to simulate sex with another man. At ten, Phase III began, during which not a single one of us blew himself/herself up in a crowded public place. No civilians were literally turned inside out via our powerful explosives. No previously funny person was reduced to a baggy pile of bloody leaking flesh, by us, during this Phase of our operation. In addition, at eleven, in Phase IV, zero (0) planes were flown into buildings.

All of this was accomplished so surreptitiously, it attracted little public notice.

During Phase V, just after lunch, while continuing to avoid the activities listed above, we were able to avoid bulldozing a single home. Furthermore, we set, on roads in every city, in every nation in the world, a total of zero (0) roadside bombs, which, not being there, did not subsequently explode, killing/maiming a total of nobody. No bombs, cluster bombs, or rockets were launched into crowded civilian neighborhoods, from which, it was observed, no post-bomb sickening momentary silences could be heard. These silences were, in all cases, followed by no unimaginable, grief-stricken bellows of rage and loss. No sleeping babies were awakened from sleep by the sudden collapse and/or bursting into flame of his/her domicile, followed by the tortured screams of his/her family members, during Phase V.

In the early afternoon (Phase VI), our membership focused on using zero (0) trained dogs to bite/terrorize naked prisoners. In addition, no stun guns, rubber batons, rubber bullets, tear gas, or real bullets were used, by our membership, on any individual, anywhere in the world. No one was forced to don a hood. No teeth were pulled in darkened rooms. Drills were not used on human flesh, nor were whips or flames. No one was reduced to hysterical tears via a series of blows to the head or body, by us. Our membership, while casting no racial or ethnic aspersions, skillfully continued not to rape, gang-rape, or sexually assault a single person. On the contrary, during this afternoon phase, many of our membership engaged in tender loving sexual acts, flirted happily, and even consoled, in a nonsexual way, individuals to whom they were attracted, putting aside their sexual feelings out of a sudden welling of empathy.

As night fell, our membership harbored no secret feelings of rage or hatred or, if they did, prayed, meditated, or discussed these feelings with a friend, until such time as the feelings abated, or were understood to be symptomatic of some deeper sadness, at which time they made silent promises to continue to struggle with these feelings.

It should be noted that, in addition to the above-listed and planned activities completed by our members, a number of unplanned activities were completed, by part-time members, or even nonmembers.

In Chitral, Pakistan, for example, a new Al Qaeda recruit remembered an elderly American woman who had once made him laugh with a snide remark about an ugly lampshade, and the way that, as she made the remark, she touched his arm, like a mother. In Gaza, an Israeli soldier and a young Palestinian exchanged a brief look of mutual shame. In London, a bitter homophobic grandfather whose grocery bag broke open gave a loaf of very nice bread to a balding gay man who stopped to help him. A stooped toothless woman in Tokyo pounded her head with her hands, tired beyond belief of her life-long feelings of anger and negativity, and silently prayed that her heart would somehow miraculously be opened before it was too late. In Syracuse, New York, holding the broken body of his kitten, a man wept.

Who are we? A word about our membership.

Since the world began, we have gone about our work quietly, resisting the urge to generalize, insisting upon valuing the individual over the group, the actual over the conceptual, the inherent sweetness of a peaceful moment over the theoretically peaceful future supposedly to be obtained via murder or massacre. Many of us have trouble sleeping, and lie awake at night, worrying about something catastrophic befalling someone we love. We rise in the morning with no plans to convert anyone via beating, humiliation, murder, or invasion. To tell the truth, we are tired. We work. We would just like some peace and quiet. When wrong, we think about it awhile, then apologize. We stand under awnings during urban thunderstorms, moved to thoughtfulness by the beautiful, troubled, umbrella-tinged faces rushing by. In moments of crisis, we pat one another awkwardly on the back, mumbling shy truisms. Rushing to an appointment, remembering a friend who has passed away, our eyes well with tears and we think: Well, my God, I was lucky just to have known him.

This is us. This is who we are. This is PRKA. To those who would oppose us, I would simply say: We are many. We are worldwide. We, in fact, outnumber you. Though you are louder, though you create a momentary ripple on the water of life, we will endure, and prevail.

Join us.

Resistance is futile.

ACKNOWLEDGMENTS

I'm opposed to long gushy Acknowledgments. But life is short, and the older I get, the more grateful I am. So here goes:

I'd like to thank Geoffrey Kloske, the great Sean McDonald (the quiet master of the Excellent Counsel, an untiring advocate for my writing), Larissa Dooley, Heather Connor, Craig Burke, Benjamin Gibson, Rodrigo Corral, Michael Schmelling, Jennifer Eck, Kimberly Johnson, and everybody else at Riverhead Books, which is the literary home I dreamed of long ago when I started writing; At ICM: the great Esther Newberg, Josie Freedman, Chris Earle, Liz Farrell, Kari Stuart, Michael McCarthy, Buddy Thomas, and Kate Jones, who represent me as if they were me, if I were better at math and not such a pushover; David Remnick, Deborah Treisman, Susan Morrison, Rhonda Sherman, and my whole beloved extended family at the *New Yorker*; Jim Nelson, Andy Ward (my guide through the travel pieces, a phenom of generosity and positive vision), Ben Phelan, Greg Veis, Raha Naddaf, and everyone at *GQ* for making the last two years such a surprise and a delight; thanks to Caitlin Saunders for the author photo; all of the great people at Bloomsbury: Alexandra Pringle, Mike Jones, and Anya Rosenberg; Merope Mills and Bob Granleese and everyone at the *Guardian*; Meghan O'Rourke at *Slate*; the generous people, too many to name here, who helped me on my *GQ* trips, especially: (in Nepal) the wonderful Subel Bhandari and (along the Mexican border): Katie Founds,

Dan Garibay, John and Abby Garland, Karen Spicher, Melissa Barkin, the "Rodriguez family" (you know who you are), Lupe Aguilar, Sam Tyx, Cynta de Narvaez, and the Minutemen, especially Al.

I'd also like to thank my colleagues and students (past, current, and future) in the Syracuse University Creative Writing Program: the greatest place to teach in the world, in no small part because of the unfailing support of the College of Arts and Sciences and our Dean, Cathryn Newton.

Also, I would like to thank the MacArthur Foundation, the Guggenheim Foundation, and the Lannan Foundation: it would be impossible to overstate how much your generous support has meant to me and my family.

On the personal front, I'd like to acknowledge and thank my sisters Nancy (who did such a great thing for NM) and Jane (my funny pal, aka Hane, who is very sentimental, and is probably crying right now as she reads this); Joe and Sheri Lindbloom, who did so much to teach me early on that ideas mattered, and especially my grandmother Marie Saunders, who has been, since my earliest memory, a model of loving kindness. I'd also like to thank my best friend, Pat Pacino. We've debated and discussed and developed many of the ideas in this book over the years, in various places and contexts, and I'm grateful to have such a dedicated, brilliant friend. Let us chicken-walk together, vigorously debating, to the grave, but not yet.

Finally, unending thanks to Paula, Caitlin, and Alena, who not only encouraged me to do the trips described in this book, but in one case even *forced* me (thanks, Alena), then listened lovingly to my incoherent ramblings afterward. These were beautiful, life-changing experiences that wouldn't have been anywhere near as wonderful if I hadn't known that the three of you were waiting for me at home, rooting for me.

And although I've thanked you above, and because I could never thank you enough: Paula, Paula, Paula. Odd to thank the air one breathes, but crazy not to.

Other Ridiculously Good Books by George Saunders

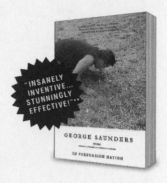

In Persuasion Nation
ISBN 978-1-59448-242-7

The Brief and Frightening Reign of Phil
ISBN 978-1-59448-152-9

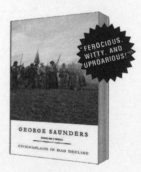

Pastoralia
ISBN 978-1-57322-872-5

CivilWarLand in Bad Decline
ISBN 978-1-57322-579-3

*Sam Lipsyte, Bookforum   ** The New York Times Book Review   † The Austin Chronicle   †† The Boston Globe*

RIVERHEAD BOOKS